Sweet **Vegan**

Sweet Vegan

A Collection of ALL VEGAN, SOME GLUTEN-FREE, AND A FEW RAW *Desserts*

Emily Mainquist

Photography by Penny de los Santos

Kyle Books

Published in 2011 by Kyle Books,
an imprint of Kyle Cathie Ltd.
www.kylebooks.com

Distributed by National Book Network
4501 Forbes Blvd., Suite 200
Lanham, MD 20706
Phone: (800) 462-6420 Fax: (301) 429-5746
custserv@nbnbooks.com

Text © 2011 Emily Mainquist
Photography © 2011 Penny de los Santos
Book design © 2011 Kyle Cathie Limited

Project editor Anja Schmidt
Designer Rita Sowins/Sowins Design
Photographer Penny de los Santos
Food Styling Susan Vajaranat
Prop Styling Audrey Weppler
Copyeditor Helen Chin
Production Lisa Pinnell and Gemma John

ISBN 978-1-906868-35-2

Library of Congress Control Number: 2010938774

Color reproduction by Sang Choy International
Printed and bound in China by Toppan Printing Co, Ltd.

✸ Contents ✸

farmsanctuary
rescue • education • advocacy

Thank you for picking up this book and for exploring the world of tasty vegan desserts. As Emily so wonderfully demonstrates, vegan sweets can be both delicious and easy to make. You'll love making and eating these treats and you can feel good in knowing that animals were not made to suffer for your eating pleasure.

Sweet Vegan is an excellent contribution to a burgeoning food movement. It comes amidst growing evidence about how factory farming threatens human health, the environment, and the well-being of animals. More and more people are changing how they eat. Restaurants and grocery stores across the U.S. are offering a wide variety of vegan foods, and amazing cookbooks like Emily's *Sweet Vegan* are providing recipes and advice for people who want to cook or prepare raw dishes at home. People are rediscovering the art of food preparation and the joy that comes with creating and sharing tasty morsels with friends, family, and loved ones. And the positive experience is enhanced when the food is cruelty free.

As we think about our food choices and endeavor to live in a way that is humane, healthy, and environmentally sustainable, we must inevitably move toward consuming plant foods in place of animal products. Alternatives to meat, dairy, and eggs are hitting the marketplace, and chefs of all stripes are getting creative in the kitchen. In *Sweet Vegan*, Emily provides wonderful recipes for you to try along with helpful advice about plant-based substitutes for dairy and eggs.

It doesn't make sense to support a food system that causes unnecessary violence and environmental destruction, especially when there are healthy plant-based alternatives that can satisfy every gustatory desire. Emily has produced a wonderful book that shows how enjoyable vegan desserts can be, and in addition to satisfying your taste buds, the dishes included here will also sit well with your conscience.

—*Gene Baur, Watkins Glen, NY, August 2010*

 **INTRODUCTION**

So Why Vegan?

If you picked up this cookbook you may be asking yourself why vegan? There are many reasons. Vegan means loving animals and, by not consuming any animal products, letting them live a healthy enjoyable life on this earth just as we do. Vegan means taking care of the environment—all the transportation in the world combined doesn't equal the greenhouse gases produced by livestock on factory farms. And 70% of the grain grown in the United States is used to feed animals on factory farms, food that could go a long way to feeding starving people around the world. Vegan also means being healthy; when I made the switch, I felt better, had more energy, and didn't need to worry about my weight or cholesterol. Being vegan is better for animals, the earth, and ourselves!

Growing up in my Italian family, everything revolved around food. I didn't play games or watch TV like other kids my age. I was in the kitchen, baking with my mom: breads, cannoli, rum cake, peach biscuits, and all kinds of Italian cookies. I remember standing on a chair when I was too short to reach the counter and measuring the flour and sugar for a batch of cookies. It was so exciting to see the results of my hard work and nothing beat eating the cookies fresh out of the oven. My mom was known for her desserts and loved to give them away to the mailman, neighbors, the electrician that came by to fix some wires at her house—it didn't matter who they were, it was her joy to give people great-tasting desserts.

I share that passion for brightening someone's day with baked goods. My plan was to go to culinary school and become a pastry chef. I needed a portfolio to apply, so I started a "business" out of my parents' house, putting menus for desserts in our neighbors' mailboxes. Soon I was getting orders from the local car dealerships and hair salons. People were enjoying my desserts so much, I decided to forego culinary school and figure out a way to establish and expand my business into a full-time job.

Turning Vegan

Meanwhile, it took an insensitive former boss to open my eyes to animal testing and factory farming. Like many people, I was ignorant to the fact that animals are treated cruelly for testing human products. When I came across what was done to animals by factory farming, I was so disgusted that I turned vegetarian that day and never looked back.

Becoming vegan took a little more time. It involved a whole new way of thinking about food. For me, like many vegans, cheese was the most difficult animal product to give up. But once I was able to convince myself that I didn't need cheese or butter or milk to make my food taste good, it was easy to go vegan. And now I don't miss those ingredients at all. There are so many substitutes that there really is no excuse not to use them.

Determined to stick to a new lifestyle, I decided to turn one of my cookie recipes vegan. I bought all the vegan ingredients I could find, and after several attempts, I brought my first batch of vegan cookies into work: Oatmeal Cherry Chocolate Pecan to be exact. It wasn't out of the ordinary for me to bring in goodies, and, without telling anyone that the cookies were vegan, I gave them out throughout the office. Later I explained the cookies didn't have any eggs or dairy in them and everyone was so surprised. No one could tell that the cookies were vegan. With these rave reviews, I realized that I may be on to something.

Founding Emily's Desserts

One of my co-workers, who was also vegetarian, took some of the cookies into a local natural foods store. The owner of the store loved the cookies and wanted to carry them. So the idea of a vegan Emily's Desserts was born. Never in my wildest dreams did I think about selling my desserts in a grocery store. Online maybe, but getting them to the mass market was just a dream come true. Since then I've opened my first retail kiosk and have collaborated with a vegan wine supplier to pair my cupcakes with wine. Making vegan desserts has happily become my full-time job!

It's incredibly rewarding to see someone who is vegan, or someone who has a dairy or egg allergy, eat my desserts. I know how hard it is to find delicious desserts that are cruelty free. I love seeing people's smiles of surprise at how good a vegan cookie, or cake, can taste. In the end, I did not go to culinary school, and you might say that's life throwing me a curve ball, but my life story has unfolded into exciting and unforeseen experiences and challenges. My story had to happen the way it did for me to become vegan and want to make a difference for vegan cooks everywhere. With *Sweet Vegan*, I prove that vegan is absolutely delectable—and better for you.

The easiest way to someone's heart is through food. Food is a universal language that everyone can relate to. *Sweet Vegan* will help you make delicious desserts to share with your friends and family. The recipes are no fuss and I have included a list below of my favorite substitutions for dairy and eggs, all of which are available online or at your local health food store.

You no longer have to sacrifice taste for what you believe in.

So why not vegan?

PREFERRED VEGAN PRODUCTS

Butter substiute: Earth Balance® Buttery Sticks™

Egg replacer: Ener-G® Egg Replacer™

Gluten-free chocolate chips: Enjoy Life® chocolate chips

Vegan marshmallows: Sweet & Sara® Marshmallows

Cream cheese substitute: Tofutti® Better Than Cream Cheese®

Sour cream substitute: Tofutti® Sour Cream

Whipped cream substitute: Soyatoo®

Evaporated cane juice (unprocessed sugar): Wholesome Sweeteners®

GLUTEN-FREE FLOUR MIX

After many cupcake rocks and cakes that felt like bricks, I found a flour combination that makes fluffy and moist gluten-free cakes. This recipe is easily substituted in most recipes that call for all-purpose flour.

 **MAKES 3 CUPS**

2 cups white rice flour
⅔ cup potato starch
⅓ cup tapioca starch
1½ teaspoons xanthan gum

Combine all the ingredients and store in an airtight container in the refrigerator for up to 90 days.

APPLE CHIPS

Apple chips are a versitile sweet that can be used as a garnish for a dessert, a topping on a salad, or snacked on right from the pan. A delicious and crunchy treat.

 MAKES 24

3 medium Granny Smith apples
½ cup organic powdered sugar

1. Preheat the oven to 250°F. Line a 10 x 15-inch cookie tray with aluminum foil.
2. Thinly slice the apples and dip them in the powdered sugar. Place the prepared cookie tray and bake for 20 to 25 minutes, or until the apples are golden brown. Cool and store in an airtight container.

COCONUT WHIPPED CREAM

A very easy whipped cream substitute, this recipe has a light and creamy texture with a slight coconut flavor. Delicious as a topping for dessert or with fresh berries.

 MAKES 2 CUPS

Two 8-ounce cans coconut milk
¼ to ½ cup organic powdered sugar

1. Store cans of high-fat coconut milk in the refrigerator at least 8 hours before use. Once chilled, open the cans, making sure not to tilt them over. Remove the lid and scrape the top layer of the coconut fat from the milk layer. Place the coconut fat into a stand mixer. Beat on low speed for 20 seconds. Add the powdered sugar and whip on high for 10 seconds. The mixture will be lumpy.
2. Place in the refrigerator to firm for 1 hour. Whip with a large whisk until the lumps are removed. Serve immediately.

✸ Breakfast Sweets ✸

✳ RECIPE LIST ✳

GRANOLA

This granola recipe is the best you will ever taste—just ask my grandmom. The coconut and cinnamon add a richness to the slightly sweet oats. Also delicious over soy yogurt with fresh fruit.

4 cups old-fashioned oats

½ cup unsweetened coconut

1 cup whole raw almonds

½ cup dark brown sugar

½ teaspoon salt

1 teaspoon cinnamon

¼ cup vegetable oil

¼ cup light agave

1 teaspoon vanilla extract

1½ cups raisins

1. Preheat the oven to 300°F.
2. In a large bowl, mix the oats, coconut, almonds, brown sugar, salt, and cinnamon.
3. Heat the oil and agave in a microwave-safe bowl for 20 seconds. Pour over the oat mixture. Add the vanilla extract and stir until combined. Spread the granola onto a 9x13-inch baking pan.
4. Bake for 40 minutes, stirring every 10 minutes. Place the pan on a wire rack, stir in the raisins, and push the granola to one side of the pan while cooling. This will allow the granola to cool in large clusters. Keep the granola in an airtight container for up to 1 month.

BLUEBERRY MUFFINS

 **MAKES 8 TO 10**

The cinnamon in these muffins complements the blueberries and adds a depth of flavor to an otherwise basic recipe. Spread some vegan butter on muffins fresh out of the oven—so delicious.

1½ cups unbleached flour

¾ cup evaporated cane juice

½ teaspoon cinnamon

2 teaspoons baking powder

½ teaspoon salt

⅓ cup vegetable oil

⅓ cup soy milk

3 teaspoons egg replacer, whisked with 4 tablespoons warm water

2 teaspoons vanilla extract

1 cup fresh blueberries

1. Preheat the oven to 350°F. Line 8 to 10 standard-size muffin cavities with paper liners.

2. In a large bowl, mix the flour, cane juice, cinnamon, baking powder, and salt. Add the oil, soy milk, egg replacer, and vanilla extract and mix until well combined. Fold in the blueberries. The batter will be very thick.

3. Scoop ¼ cup of batter into each muffin liner. Bake for 18 to 20 minutes, or until a toothpick inserted in the center of a muffin comes out clean.

BANANA WALNUT MUFFINS

 MAKES 8

My husband loves these muffins so much that I make them for him at least three days a week for a mid-morning snack. It's all about taste combined with texture here: the sweet banana mixes with the hearty walnut crunch for a healthy breakfast that tastes like dessert!

2 cups unbleached flour

¾ cup evaporated cane juice

1 teaspoon baking soda

½ teaspoon salt

½ cup butter substitute

3 ripe bananas (about 1 cup)

3 teaspoons egg replacer, whisked with 4 tablespoons warm water

1 teaspoon vanilla extract

¾ cup chopped walnuts

1. Preheat the oven to 350°F. Line 8 standard-size muffin cavities with paper liners.

2. In a large bowl, mix the flour, cane juice, baking soda, and salt.

3. Melt the butter substitute in a microwave-safe bowl. Using a food processor or the back of a spoon, blend or mash the bananas until they are pureed. Add the melted butter substitute, bananas, egg replacer, vanilla extract, and chopped walnuts to the large bowl and mix until well combined. The batter will be very thick.

4. Scoop ¼ cup batter into each muffin liner. Bake the muffins for 18 to 20 minutes, or until a toothpick inserted in the center of a muffin comes out clean.

CINNAMON CRANBERRY MUFFINS

 MAKES 8

The flavor combination of this muffin is truly unique: The spice from the cinnamon mixed with the tartness of the cranberries will make your taste buds sing. Dab with vegan butter and sprinkle with cinnamon sugar for an extra rich treat.

1½ cups unbleached flour

¾ cup evaporated cane juice

2 teaspoons cinnamon

2 teaspoons baking powder

½ teaspoon salt

⅓ cup vegetable oil

⅓ cup soy milk

3 teaspoons egg replacer, whisked with 4 tablespoons warm water

2 teaspoons vanilla extract

¾ cup dried cranberries

1. Preheat the oven to 350°F. Line 8 standard-size muffin cavities with paper liners.
2. In a large bowl, mix the flour, cane juice, cinnamon, baking powder, and salt. Add the oil, soy milk, egg replacer, and vanilla extract and mix until well combined. Fold in the cranberries. The batter will be very thick.
3. Scoop ¼ cup batter into each muffin liner. Bake the muffins for 18 to 20 minutes, or until a toothpick inserted in the center of a muffin comes out clean.

✳ *Gluten-Free* ✳ CHOCOLATE-CHIP ZUCCHINI BREAD SQUARES

SERVES 8

When I was growing up, my Aunt Trisha would often make this sweet bread. Her secret was to add lots of chocolate chips. I've adapted her recipe to make it both vegan and gluten free. This bread is still as moist and delicious as my Aunt Trisha's and now everyone can enjoy it.

4 tablespoons butter substitute, at room temperature

⅔ cup dark brown sugar

1 teaspoon vanilla extract

1 cup Gluten-Free Flour Mix (page 13)

1 teaspoon baking soda

½ teaspoon salt

1 teaspoon cinnamon

½ cup chopped walnuts

1 cup finely shredded zucchini, drained

1½ teaspoons egg replacer, whisked with 2 tablespoons warm water

½ cup gluten-free chocolate chips

1. Preheat the oven to 350°F. Grease and flour an 8 x 8-inch baking pan.

2. In a stand mixer, beat the butter substitute with the brown sugar and vanilla extract until light and fluffy, about 2 minutes on medium speed. Stop and scrape down the sides of bowl then add the flour, baking soda, salt, cinnamon, walnuts, and zucchini. Mix on medium speed for 30 seconds. Stop and scrape down the sides of bowl. Add the egg replacer mixture and chocolate chips and mix for another 30 seconds.

3. Spread the batter onto the prepared baking pan. Bake for 25 to 30 minutes, or until a toothpick inserted in the center comes out clean. Cool on a wire rack at least 1 hour before cutting into squares.

MONKEY BREAD

Monkey Bread is like a compilation of mini pull-apart cinnamon rolls. Some might remember this dessert from Girl Scout days. I remember making it as a kid with my mom on winter days when school was out due to snow. This is delicious served with chai tea or hazelnut coffee.

BISCUITS

6 cups unbleached flour

6 teaspoons baking powder

1½ teaspoons salt

12 tablespoons butter substitute

2¼ cups soy milk

CINNAMON DIPPING SAUCE

4 tablespoons cinnamon

2 cups evaporated cane juice

1 cup butter substitute, melted

1½ cups light brown sugar

GLAZE

1 cup organic powdered sugar

2 tablespoons water

1. Preheat the oven to 350°F.
2. FIRST MAKE THE BISCUITS: Using a stand mixer, combine the flour, baking powder, and salt on low speed. With the motor still running, add the butter substitute 1 tablespoon at a time, waiting 5 seconds after each addition, until a soft dough is formed. Add the soy mik and beat the dough on medium speed until a soft dough forms, about 20 seconds.
3. Mix the cinnamon and cane juice in a small bowl and set aside. On a lightly floured work surface, roll the dough to 1 inch thick and cut into 1-inch squares. Roll each square into a ball and dip in the melted butter substitute, then in the cinnamon sugar mixture. Place each ball into a bundt pan, arranging in even layers, working up the sides of the pan.
4. In a microwave-safe bowl, melt the butter substitute for 1 minute, then stir until completely melted. Add the brown sugar and stir until combined. Pour over the cinnamon sugar biscuits in the bundt pan.
5. Bake for 35 to 40 minutes until golden brown. Cool in the pan on a wire rack for 10 minutes. Invert the pan to release the Monkey Bread. Cool for 30 minutes more.
6. Meanwhile, whisk the powdered sugar and water until combined. Drizzle over the cooled Monkey Bread before serving.

PEACH BISCUITS

MAKES 10

My mom always made peach biscuits for summer barbecues when I was a kid. We picked peaches from a peach farm in Pennsylvania and, when we got home, I helped her cut the biscuits and dip them into the butter and cinnamon sugar. So delicious on a hot summer day, these biscuits are great served for brunch or dessert.

BISCUITS

2 cups unbleached flour

2 teaspoons baking powder

½ teaspoon salt

4 tablespoons butter substitute

¾ cup soy milk

FRUIT TOPPING

4 large peaches

3 tablespoons apricot preserves

1 tablespoon water

COATING

1 cup evaporated cane juice

2 teaspoons cinnamon

1½ cups butter substitute

1. Preheat the oven to 375°F.
2. FIRST MAKE THE BISCUITS: Using a stand mixer, combine the flour, baking powder, and salt on medium speed. With the motor still running, add the butter substitute 1 tablespoon at a time, waiting 5 seconds after each addition. Add the soy milk and beat the dough on medium speed until a soft dough has formed. Turn the dough out onto a lightly floured work surface, and roll to ½ inch thick. Cut with a 4-inch round cookie cutter. Take any remaining biscuit dough and roll out and cut until you can't cut any more biscuits. Set aside.
3. Wash and dry the peaches and cut into ¼-inch-thick slices. Set aside.
4. To make the coating, mix the cane juice and cinnamon in a medium bowl. Melt the butter substitute in a microwave-safe bowl for 1 minute. Dip the biscuits into the melted butter, then in the cinnamon sugar, and place on a 10 x 15-inch cookie tray.
5. Create a well in each biscuit. Arrange the sliced peaches, slightly overlapping, in each well. Sprinkle with any remaining cinnamon sugar.
6. Bake for 12 to 15 minutes, or until golden. Cool on a wire rack for 5 minutes. Meanwhile, melt the apricot preserves with the water in a microwave-safe dish for 20 seconds, then spread onto the still-warm biscuits before serving.

CINNAMON CRUMB CAKE

 SERVES 12

This cake is definitely a classic that cried out for a yummy vegan version. The combination of moist yellow cake swirled with cinnamon and topped with a buttery brown sugar topping—how much better can it get? Cinnamon Crumb Cake is always fantastic with coffee and great conversation.

CRUMB TOPPING

1 cup unbleached flour

½ cup light brown sugar

1 teaspoon cinnamon

½ cup butter substitute

CAKE

1 cup butter substitute, at room temperature

1½ cups evaporated cane juice

2 teaspoons vanilla extract

3 cups unbleached flour

4 teaspoons baking powder

2 tablespoons cinnamon

6 teaspoons egg replacer, whisked with 8 tablespoons warm water

1 cup soy milk

1 tablespoon white vinegar

Organic powdered sugar, for finishing

1. Preheat the oven to 350°F. Grease and flour a 9x13-inch baking pan.
2. FIRST MAKE THE CRUMB TOPPING: In a stand mixer, combine the flour, brown sugar, and cinnamon on medium speed. With the motor still running, add the butter substitute 1 tablespoon at a time. Continue mixing until the topping resembles very coarse sand. Set aside.
3. Using a stand mixer, beat the butter substitute, cane juice, and vanilla extract until combined. Stop and scrape down the sides of the bowl, then turn the mixer to high speed and whip the mixture until it's light and fluffy, about 2 minutes.
4. In a small bowl, mix the flour, baking powder, and cinnamon. In a separate bowl, combine the egg replacer with the soy milk and vinegar. Alternate adding the dry and wet ingredients, starting and ending with the dry ingredients, to the mixer bowl. After each addition, beat for 10 seconds at medium speed and stop and scrape down the sides of bowl, making sure that all the butter substitute is incorporated. Beat an additional 30 seconds.
5. Spread the batter into the prepared baking pan and sprinkle with all of the crumb topping. Bake the cake for 45 to 50 minutes, or until a cake tester comes out clean. Sprinkle with powdered sugar.

CINNAMON ROLLS

You will not be disappointed with this recipe. The rolls come out rich and gooey, just like the ones from your childhood. I sell these in stores and can't keep them on the shelves. Nothing is better on a weekend than the smell of cinnamon rolls in the morning.

¼ cup plus 1 tablespoon warm water

1 cup soy milk

2½ teaspoons active dry yeast

1½ cups evaporated cane juice

4½ cups bread flour

3 teaspoons egg replacer, mixed with 4 tablespoons warm water

1 teaspoon salt

5 tablespoons butter substitute, melted

FILLING

1 cup dark brown sugar

2 teaspoons cinnamon

⅓ cup butter substitute, softened

Cream Cheese Frosting (page 66)

1. Preheat the oven to 375°F.

2. Warm the soy milk in a microwave-safe bowl for 30 seconds. Place the yeast into the bowl of a stand mixer. Pour in the warm soy milk and let the yeast activate for about 2 minutes. Add the cane juice, flour, and egg replacer to the bowl. With a dough hook, mix on medium speed, adding the salt and melted butter substitute after 10 seconds. Continue to mix until the dough is formed and kneaded by the machine, about 5 minutes more. Place the dough in a large greased bowl and cover with a kitchen towel or plastic wrap. Let rise for 1 hour in a warm place, until doubled in size.

3. Meanwhile, in a small bowl, combine the brown sugar and cinnamon. Set aside.

4. Once the dough is ready to roll, lightly flour your work surface and rolling pin. Roll the dough into a 16 x 21-inch rectangle, a ½ inch thick. Spread the softened butter in an even layer on top. Sprinkle with the brown sugar, cinnamon, and cane juice. Roll the dough lengthwise as tight as possible. Using a serrated knife, cut each roll 1½ inches thick and place in a 9x13-inch baking pan. Place on a 9 x 13-inch backing pan. Cover with a kitchen towel or plastic wrap and let rise until doubled in size, about 30 minutes.

5. Bake the cinnamon rolls for 12 to 14 minutes until golden brown. Spread or drizzle with the cream cheese frosting. Serve immediately.

PUMPKIN ROLL

 **SERVES 8 TO 10**

This dessert has always been a classic at our house in the fall. A perfect addition to your Thanksgiving dessert table, it's also great with spiced apple cider.

¾ cup unbleached flour

1 cup evaporated cane juice

1 teaspoon baking soda

¾ teaspoon cinnamon

4½ teaspoons egg replacer, whisked with 6 tablespoons warm water

⅔ cup pumpkin puree

½ cup organic powdered sugar

CREAM CHEESE FILLING

6 tablespoons butter substitute, at room temperature

8 ounces tofu cream cheese, at room temperature

1 teaspoon vanilla extract

3 cups organic powdered sugar, plus two tablespoons for finishing

1. Preheat the oven to 350°F. Grease and flour a 10x15-inch cookie sheet.

2. Using a stand mixer, combine the flour, cane juice, baking soda, and cinnamon. Add the egg replacer and pumpkin and beat for 30 seconds on medium speed. Spread in the prepared cookie sheet.

3. Bake for 10 to 12 minutes, or until a toothpick inserted in the center of the cakes comes out clean. Flip the cake out onto a hand towel that has been sprinkled with the powdered sugar. Roll the cake and towel together widthwise in a jellyroll fashion. Let cool for 30 minutes.

4. MEANWHILE, MAKE THE CREAM CHEESE FILLING: In a stand mixer, beat the butter substitute and cream cheese at medium speed until smooth, about 2 minutes. Stop and scrape down the sides of the bowl. Add the vanilla extract and mix on medium speed for 20 seconds. With the motor still running, add the 3 cups powdered sugar 1 cup at a time, stopping and scraping down the sides of the bowl after each addition. Whip the frosting for 1 minute more on high speed.

5. Unroll the cooked pumpkin cake and spread the frosting evenly on top. Re-roll the cake without the towel and refrigerate for 2 hours before serving. Dust with the 2 tablespoons of powdered sugar right before serving.

☀ Sweets in Crusts ☀

✳ RECIPE LIST ✳

DUTCH APPLE PIE

Dutch apple pie has been around for centuries—probably because everyone loves the flavorings of cinnamon and lemon juice with the tart apples. Dutch apple pies are traditionally finished with a crisp lattice top, but I like to use a sweet crumb topping.

CRUST

⅓ cup non-hydrogenated shortening

1¼ cups unbleached flour

¼ teaspoon salt

4 tablespoons cold water

APPLE FILLING

6 large Granny Smith apples

¼ cup unbleached flour

¾ cup evaporated cane juice

2 teaspoons cinnamon

CRUMB TOPPING

1 cup unbleached flour

½ cup brown sugar

8 tablespoons butter substitute

1. Preheat the oven to 425°F.

2. MAKE THE CRUST: Using a standing mixer, beat the shortening on medium speed until smooth. Scrape down the sides of the bowl and add the flour and salt. While the mixer is still running, add the cold water one tablespoon at a time until a dough starts to form. Blend the mixture until just combined, 30 seconds. (Blending too much will make the dough tough.) On a lightly floured work surface, roll out the dough to ¼ inch thick. Roll the dough onto a rolling pin and unroll it into a pie plate. Crimp the edges of the dough and set aside.

3. MAKE THE APPLE FILLING: Peel, core, and thinly slice the apples to ¼ inch thick. In a large bowl, mix the flour, cane juice, and cinnamon with the apple slices. Set aside.

4. MAKE THE CRUMB TOPPING: In a standing mixer, combine the flour and brown sugar. While the mixer was still running, add the butter substitute 1 tablespoon at a time. Mix until the crumb topping resembles very coarse sand.

5. Spoon the apples from the large bowl into the pie crust, making sure not to get the liquid from the bowl into the pie crust (this will help the pie to stay together once cut). Top with all of the crumb topping. Place the pie plate on a foil-lined baking sheet for easy cleanup. Cover the pie with foil and bake for 35 minutes. Turn down the heat to 350°F, remove the foil, and bake for 10 more minutes to brown the topping and crust. Cool on a wire rack for 1 hour. Lightly cover at room temperature to store.

APPLE CHEESECAKE TART

 **SERVES 8 TO 10**

This dessert is a combination of cheesecake and apple pie—and a unique result of one of my brainstorming sessions. It is a delicious mix of smooth vanilla filling and crisp cinnamon apples. I love to add the beautiful garnish of apple chips; the recipe can be found at the end of the introduction to this book.

CRUST

⅓ cup non-hydrogenated shortening

1¼ cups plus 2 tablespoons unbleached flour

¼ teaspoon salt

4 tablespoons cold water

CHEESECAKE FILLING

8 ounces tofu cream cheese, at room temperature

⅔ cup tofu sour cream

⅓ cup evaporated cane juice

1 teaspoon vanilla extract

1½ teaspoons egg replacer, whisked with 2 tablespoons warm water

1. Preheat the oven to 350°F.

2. FIRST MAKE THE CRUST: Using a stand mixer, beat the shortening on medium speed until smooth. Add the flour and salt, blending until combined, about 20 seconds. Add the cold water 1 tablespoon at a time, mixing after each addition. Continue mixing until a soft dough is formed, about 30 seconds. (Blending too much will make the dough tough.) On a lightly floured work surface, roll out the dough to ¼ inch thick. Prick all over with a fork. Roll the dough around a rolling pin and then unroll into a 9-inch tart pan. Press against the bottom and sides of the pan, cutting away any extra dough. Bake for 15 minutes, then remove from the oven and set aside.

3. MEANWHILE, MAKE THE CHEESECAKE FILLING: Using a stand mixer, beat the cream cheese on medium-high speed until smooth. Stop and scrape down the sides of the bowl, then add the sour cream, cane juice, and vanilla extract to the bowl. Mix the filling on medium speed for about 1 minute, stopping and scraping down the sides of the bowl as necessary. In a small bowl, whisk the egg replacer and water until frothy, add to the mixing bowl and whip for an additional 30 seconds on high speed. Spread evenly into the cooled crust.

4. To make the apple filling, peel, core, and slice the apples ¼ inch thick. In a medium bowl, mix the apples with the cane juice and cinnamon. Arrange the apples on top of the cheesecake filling in a single layer.

APPLE FILLING

3 medium Granny Smith apples

¼ cup evaporated cane juice

1 teaspoon cinnamon

CRUMB TOPPING

½ cup flour

¼ cup organic brown sugar

⅓ cup chopped pecans

5 tablespoons butter substitute

APPLE CHIPS, for garnish
(see page 13)

8 to 10 cinnamon sticks

5. MAKE THE CRUMP TOPPING: Using a stand mixer, combine the flour, sugar, and pecans. With the motor running on medium speed, add the butter substitute in 1 tablespoon additions, waiting 10 seconds between each addition. Continue beating until the mixture resembles coarse sand, about 30 seconds, but watch closely to avoid the topping turning into one large clump. Sprinkle the crumb topping on top of the apples.

6. Bake the tart for 40 to 45 minutes until golden brown. Cool for at least 3 hours in the refrigerator before cutting. Garnish each slice with an Apple Chip and a cinnamon stick. Store any leftover tart in the refrigerator for up to a week.

APPLE CRISP

I include dried cherries in this beloved dessert to add a slightly tart burst of flavor to the sweet apple cinnamon filling. I always use Granny Smith apples because they keep their crisp texture.

FILLING

6 cups Granny Smith apples

¼ cup unbleached flour

¾ cup evaporated cane juice

2 cups oats

2 teaspoons cinnamon

1 cup dried cherries

CRUMB TOPPING

1 cup unbleached flour

½ cup dark brown sugar

8 tablespoons butter substitute

1. Preheat the oven to 425°F.

2. To make the apple filling, peel, core and thinly slice the apples to ¼ inch thick. In a large bowl, mix the flour, cane juice, oats, cinnamon, and cherries. Add the apple slices and toss well. Set aside.

3. NEXT MAKE THE CRUMB TOPPING: In a stand mixer, combine the flour and brown sugar on medium speed. With the motor still running, add the butter substitute 1 tablespoon at a time. Continue mixing until the topping resembles very coarse sand.

4. Spoon the apple filling into a 2-quart baking dish. Top with the crumb topping. Place the dish on a foil-covered cookie sheet for easy cleanup, and cover the baking dish with foil.

5. Bake the apple crisp, covered, for 40 minutes. Remove the foil, decrease the heat to 350°F, and bake another 10 minutes, until the topping is nicely browned.

RUSTIC APPLE PIE

SERVES 12 TO 15

The overhanging and then folded-over crust for this pie gives it its rustic feel—not only a beautiful dish for the fall but an easy and delicious recipe for an abundance of apple picking.

CRUST

4 ounces tofu cream cheese, at room temperature

½ cup butter substitute, at room temperature

1½ cups unbleached flour

FILLING

4 ounces tofu cream cheese, at room temperature

3 tablespoons evaporated cane juice, divided

1¼ teaspoons cinnamon, divided

2 medium Granny Smith apples, peeled, cored, and cut into ¼-inch slices

1 teaspoon cornstarch

½ cup organic dried cranberries

GLAZE

1 cup organic powdered sugar

2 tablespoons water

1. Preheat the oven to 400°F. Line a cookie sheet with aluminum foil.

2. FIRST MAKE THE CRUST: Using a stand mixer, combine the cream cheese and butter substitute on medium speed for 2 minutes. Stop and scrape down the sides of the bowl and add the flour. Mix until well blended. Shape the dough into a ball; wrap tightly with plastic wrap and refrigerate for 1 hour. Once chilled, place the dough on a lightly floured work surface. Roll into a 14x8-inch rectangle, transfer to the prepared cookie sheet, and set aside.

3. NEXT MAKE THE FILLING: In a medium bowl, stir the cream cheese with 1 tablespoon cane juice and ½ teaspoon cinnamon. Mix until combined. Spread onto the crust within 2 inches of the edge.

4. In another bowl, toss the apple slices with 2 tablespoons cane juice, ¾ teaspoon cinnamon, and the cornstarch. Arrange on top of the cream cheese filling in a single layer. Fold the edges of the pastry in, toward the apples. Bake for 30 to 35 minutes, until the crust is golden.

5. Meanwhile, in a small bowl, whisk the powdered sugar and water until combined. Set aside.

6. Remove the pie from the oven and sprinkle the cranberries on top of it while it's hot, then let cool for 15 minutes. Drizzle with the glaze.

STRAWBERRY CHEESECAKE

The crust made from my own agave graham cracker recipe gives this strawberry cheesecake an added wow factor. You can easily substitute blueberries, peaches, or raspberries for the strawberries.

CRUST

24 Agave Graham Crackers
(page 104)

¼ cup butter substitute, melted

¼ cup evaporated cane juice

FILLING

32 ounces tofu cream cheese

6 teaspoons egg replacer, whisked with 8 tablespoons warm water

1½ cups evaporated cane juice

1 cup strawberry jam

1 cup sliced strawberries

1. Preheat the oven to 350°F. Grease and flour a 9x13-inch baking pan.
2. FIRST MAKE THE CRUST: Using a food processor, finely crush the graham crackers.
3. In a medium bowl, combine the butter substitute, graham crackers, and cane juice. Press into the prepared baking pan and set aside.
4. NEXT MAKE THE FILLING: Using a stand mixer, beat the cream cheese on medium speed until smooth, about 2 minutes, stopping and scraping down the sides of the bowl as needed. Add the egg replacer and cane juice and blend on medium-high speed for 2 minutes. Pour into the crust.
5. Bake for 40 to 45 minutes, until the center is slightly firm. Refrigerate for 8 hours or overnight.
6. Before serving, spread the strawberry jam on the cheesecake. Top with the sliced strawberries.

TRIPLE CHOCOLATE CHEESECAKE

This cheesecake is a chocoholic's dream. Crisp chocolate cookie crust, rich chocolate filling, and decadent chocolate ganache topping make up these three layers of chocolate bliss. This is extra delicious served with fresh berries.

CRUST

10 chocolate sandwich cookies

½ teaspoon ground coffee

3 tablespoons butter substitute, melted

FILLING

8 ounces tofu cream cheese, at room temperature

⅔ cup evaporated cane juice

½ cup tofu sour cream

3 teaspoons egg replacer, whisked with 4 tablespoons warm water

8 ounces gluten-free chocolate chips

CHOCOLATE GLAZE

4 ounces gluten-free chocolate chips

2 tablespoons butter substitute

1 teaspoon light agave

2 tablespoons tofu sour cream

1. Preheat the oven to 350°F.
2. MAKE THE CRUST: Finely crush the sandwich cookies in a food processor, for about 1 minute. Pour into a medium bowl and add the ground coffee. Stir in the melted butter substitute. Press the crust into a 9-inch disposable pie plate.
3. MAKE THE FILLING: Using a stand mixer, beat the cream cheese until smooth, stopping and scraping down the sides of the bowl as needed. Add the cane juice and sour cream and mix for 1 minute at medium speed. Add the egg replacer and mix for 30 seconds. Stop and scrape down the sides and bottom of the bowl.
4. In a microwave-safe bowl, melt the chocolate for 1 minute, stirring after 30 seconds. Remove from the microwave and stir until completely melted. Pour the chocolate into the mixing bowl while the motor is running, then blend on high speed for 1 minute. Pour into the crust.
5. Bake for 25 to 30 minutes until the filling slightly puffs around the edges and the center is slightly firm. Cool the pan on a wire rack for 30 minutes. Once cooled, remove the disposable pie plate and place the cheesecake on a serving dish.
6. MEANWHILE, MAKE THE GLAZE: In a microwave-safe bowl, melt the chocolate and butter substitute, about 1 minute. Add the agave and sour cream and stir until combined. Pour over the cooled cheesecake. Refrigerate at least 4 hours before serving.

PUMPKIN PIE

I turned this recipe vegan by using coconut milk, which is very similar in thickness to evaporated milk. It is a great substitute and lends a creamy texture that is delicious.

CRUST

⅓ cup non-hydrogenated shortening

1¼ cups unbleached flour

¼ teaspoon salt

4 tablespoons cold water

PUMPKIN FILLING

15-ounce can pumpkin puree

16-ounce can coconut milk

¾ cup evaporated cane juice

2 teaspoons cinnamon

½ teaspoon salt

1 teaspoon xanthan gum

3 teaspoons egg replacer

1. Preheat the oven to 400°F.

2. FIRST MAKE THE CRUST: Using a stand mixer, beat the shortening on medium speed until smooth, about 10 seconds. Add the flour and salt, blending until combined, about 30 seconds. While the mixer is still running, add the cold water one tablespoon at a time, then continue mixing until just combined, about 30 seconds more. (Blending too much will make the dough tough.)

3. Turn the dough out onto a floured work surface. Using a floured rolling pin, roll the dough ¼ inch. Roll the dough around the rolling pin and unroll it into pie plate. Cut away the extra dough and crimp the edges. Set aside.

4. MAKE THE PUMPKIN FILLING: In a large bowl, mix the pumpkin puree and coconut milk until combined. Add the cane juice, cinnamon, salt, xanthan gum, and egg replacer. Blend until well combined and pour into the crust.

5. Bake for 40 minutes or until the center of the pie is slightly firm. Cool in the pie plate for 30 minutes on a wire rack, then refrigerate for 8 hours or overnight before serving.

FRESH BERRY PIE

This simple dessert is perfect for a summer cookout when berries are in season. A light drizzle of agave gives the berries a little extra sweetness. Garnish with fresh mint and Coconut Whipped Cream (see page 13). The simple crust is used again in the recipes for Fruit Pockets (see opposite) and Fruit Pizza (see page 54).

CRUST

⅓ cup non-hydrogenated shortening

1¼ cups plus two tablespoons unbleached flour

¼ teaspoon salt

4 tablespoons cold water

BERRY FILLING

2 cups blackberries

2½ cups blueberries

2 cups raspberries

5 cups strawberries

4 tablespoons light agave

1. Preheat the oven to 425°F. Wrap the outside of a pie plate with enough aluminum foil to create an edge that is higher than the pie plate.

2. Using a stand mixer, beat the shortening on medium speed until smooth, about 10 seconds. Add the flour and salt, blending until combined, about 30 seconds. Add the cold water 1 tablespoon at a time, mixing for 10 seconds after each addition. Blend the mixture until just combined, 30 more seconds. (Blending too much will make the dough tough.)

3. Turn the dough out on a lightly floured work surface. With a lightly floured rolling pin, roll out the dough to ¼ inch thick. Prick all over with a fork. Roll the dough around the rolling pin and unroll it into the pie plate. Form the dough up the sides of the pie plate and foil. This will allow for an abstract pie shell.

4. Bake the crust for 15 minutes, then let cool on wire rack.

5. MEANWHILE, MAKE THE BERRY FILLING: Wash and dry the fruit. Cut some strawberries in half while leaving some whole. Gently stir all the fruit with the agave in a large bowl. Spoon into the cooled pie crust and serve immediately.

FRUIT POCKETS

MAKES 8 TO 10

These delicious pockets are easy to take with you to a dinner party as a gift for your host. Make them for a picnic dessert or pack them in your children's lunches for a healthier dessert at school.

CRUST

⅓ cup non-hydrogenated shortening

1¼ cups plus two tablespoons unbleached flour

¼ teaspoon salt

4 tablespoons cold water

FRUIT FILLING

2 small apples, peeled and cored

½ cups blueberries, rinsed

1 cup strawberries, rinsed

6 tablespoons evaporated cane juice

¾ cup unbleached flour

GLAZE

1 cup organic powdered sugar

2 tablespoons water

1. Preheat the oven to 425°F.

2. FIRST MAKE THE CRUST: Using a stand mixer, beat the shortening on medium speed for 10 seconds until smooth. Add the flour and salt, blending until combined, about 30 seconds. With the motor still running, add the cold water 1 tablespoon at a time until a soft dough is formed. Blend the mixture until just combined, about 30 seconds. (Blending too much will make the dough tough.) On a lightly floured work surface, roll out the dough to ¼ inch thick and cut with a 4-inch round cookie cutter. Set aside.

3. MAKE THE FRUIT FILLING: Finely chop the apples and strawberries. Cut the blueberries in half. Mix each fruit in a separate bowl with ¼ cup flour and 2 tablespoons cane juice. Spoon 1 tablespoon of the fruit mixture onto the bottom half of each circle of dough. Brush the edges of each dough circle with water and fold the top half over the filling. Crimp the edges of the dough with the tongs of a fork, and cut 2 slits at the top of each pocket—this will allow the steam to escape.

4. Bake for 12 to 15 minutes, or until browned around the edges. Cool on wire racks for 30 minutes.

5. Meanwhile, make the glaze by whisking the powdered sugar and water until combined. Pour the glaze over each fruit pocket before serving.

FRUIT PIZZA

Fresh fruit in season is the key to this dessert—and you can use any combination you like. Drizzle with melted chocolate or sprinkle with powdered sugar for an extra sweetness factor.

CRUST

⅓ cup non-hydrogenated shortening

¼ cup plus 2 tablespoons unbleached flour

¼ teaspoon salt

4 tablespoons cold water

CREAM CHEESE FILLING

6 tablespoons butter substitute, at room temperature

8 ounces tofu cream cheese

4 cups organic powdered sugar

1 teaspoon vanilla extract

FRUIT TOPPING

1 large peach

6 strawberries

1 kiwi, peeled

10 raspberries

10 blueberries

2 kumquats

2 tablespoons apricot preserves, melted

1. Preheat the oven to 375°F.

2. MAKE THE CRUST: Using a stand mixer, beat the shortening on medium speed until smooth, about 10 seconds. Stop and scrape down the sides of the bowl. Add the flour and salt, blending on medium speed until combined, about 30 seconds. Add the cold water 1 tablespoon at a time, mixing for 10 seconds after each addition. Blend the mixture once more until just combined, 30 seconds. (Blending too much will make the dough tough.) Turn the dough out onto a lightly floured work surface and roll to ¼ inch thick. Prick all over with a fork and place on a pizza stone or baking sheet. Bake until lightly golden, about 12 to 15 minutes. Cool on a wire rack.

3. MEANWHILE, MAKE THE FILLING: Using a stand mixer, beat the butter substitute on medium-high speed until smooth, about 1 minute. Stop and scrape down the sides of bowl. Add the cream cheese and mix on medium speed until combined, about 1 minute. With the motor still running, slowly add the powdered sugar. Add the vanilla extract and whip for 1 minute on high speed. Spread evenly on the cooled crust.

4. To make the fruit topping, cut all of the fruit ¼ inch thick. Arrange the fruit, overlapping, on top of the cream cheese filling. Brush the top of the fruit with the apricot preserves for a glossy finish. Store in the refrigerator for up to 2 days.

VARIATION

To make six 4-inch tarts instead of a pizza, in step 2, after rolling the dough to ¼ inch thick, cut the dough into six 4-inch diameter circles. Place each circle in a 4-inch tart pan and bake and cool as instructed above. Continue preparing the filling and fruit and, when assembling, fill each cooled tart crust with ¼ cup filling and a fruit of your choice. You can mix the fruits or keep them uniform on each tart.

CHOCOLATE CHIP COOKIE CHEESECAKE

 SERVES 8 TO 10

Two layers of rich chocolate chip cookie (this recipe uses my own packaged cookie dough, which you can find online), a smooth vanilla cheesecake filling, plus a layer of chocolate make this dessert so decadent. My Aunt Maria made this dessert when I was young and it has always been one of my favorites.

COOKIE CRUST

Three 12-ounce containers Emily's Desserts Cookie Dough

CHEESECAKE FILLING

24 ounces tofu cream cheese, at room temperature

¾ cup evaporated cane juice

4½ teaspoons egg replacer, whisked with 6 tablespoons warm water

1 teaspoon vanilla extract

Tempered chocolate, for garnish (page 132)

1. Preheat the oven to 325°F if using a dark springform pan, 350°F if using a silver springform pan.

2. FIRST MAKE THE CRUST: Thaw the cookie dough in the refrigerator overnight. Divide the dough into 2 piles, 18 ounces each. Place a large piece of plastic wrap on top of the springform pan bottom. Press half of the dough into the shape of the pan. Fold the plastic wrap around the cookie dough and flip the bottom pan over to release the dough. Repeat with the other pile of cookie dough, then place both plastic-wrapped doughs into the freezer for 15 minutes.

3. NEXT MAKE THE CHEESECAKE FILLING: Using a stand mixer, beat the cream cheese on medium-high speed until smooth, about 1 minute. Add the cane juice and vanilla extract and mix until combined. Stop and scrape down the sides of the bowl. Add the egg replacer and whip for 30 seconds on medium-high speed.

4. Unwrap one chilled cookie dough round and place it on the bottom of the springform pan. Spoon the cheesecake filling on top. Unwrap and place the second cookie dough round on top. Cover the cheesecake with aluminum foil to prevent the cookie from burning and bake for 40 minutes. Then remove the foil and bake for an additional 5 to 10 minutes until the center is slightly firm. Cool the cheesecake, wrapped in plastic in its pan, in the refrigerator for 4 to 6 hours or overnight.

5. Remove the chilled cheesecake from the refrigerator. Transfer from the pan onto a serving dish. Slice the cheesecake and dip the round end of each slice in tempered chocolate before serving.

VANILLA PUMPKIN CHEESECAKE

 **SERVES 8 TO 10**

This recipe always reminds me of autumn. The creamy vanilla and pumpkin filling on top of spicy gingersnap and walnut crust is truly delicious. Garnish with a gingersnap cookie and coconut whipped cream. Vanilla Pumpkin Cheesecake would be a great addition to any Thanksgiving or holiday dessert table.

CRUST

2½ cups crushed ginger snaps, plus 8 to 10 whole for garnish

⅓ cup pecans

6 tablespoons butter substitute, melted

VANILLA CHEESECAKE FILLING

24 ounces tofu cream cheese, at room temperature

¾ cup evaporated cane juice

1 teaspoon vanilla extract

4½ teaspoons egg replacer, whisked with 6 tablespoons warm water

PUMPKIN CHEESECAKE FILLING

1¼ cups Vanilla Cheesecake Filling

1 cup canned pumpkin puree

¼ cup evaporated cane juice

2 teaspoons cinnamon

1 teaspoon pumpkin pie spice

Coconut Whipped Cream, for garnish (see page 13)

1. Preheat the oven to 300°F if using a dark springform pan, or 325°F if using a silver springform pan.

2. MAKE THE CRUST: Grind the ginger snaps in a food processor until they are finely crushed. Add the pecans and process until just combined. Add the melted butter substitute and mix well. Press firmly onto the bottom and 1½ inches up the sides of a springform pan.

3. NEXT MAKE THE VANILLA CHEESECAKE FILLING: Using a stand mixer, blend the cream cheese on medium-high speed until smooth, about 20 seconds. Add the cane juice and mix on medium speed until combined, about 1 minute. Add the vanilla extract and whip for 30 seconds on high speed. Stop and scrape down the sides of the bowl. Add the egg replacer and beat just until blended. Reserve 1¼ cups of the filling in a medium bowl.

4. To make the pumpkin cheesecake filling, combine the reserved 1¼ cups vanilla cheesecake filling, pumpkin puree, cane juice, cinnamon, and pumpkin pie spice.

5. Spoon half of the vanilla cheesecake into the crust. Top with spoonfuls of pumpkin filling and vanilla filling in repeating layers. Run a knife through the fillings to create a marbled effect. Bake for 45 to 50 minutes, until the center is almost set. Cheesecake should be custard-like in texture so do not overbake!

6. Run a small knife between the cheesecake and the pan to loosen the cake, making sure to let it cool before removing from the pan. Refrigerate for at least 4 hours, overnight is best. Garnish each slice with a small dollop of coconut whipped cream and a gingersnap cookie.

✴ Cakes of all Kinds ✴

❋ RECIPE LIST ❋

YELLOW CAKE WITH CHOCOLATE SOUR CREAM FROSTING

SERVES 8 TO 10

I took a classic "Birthday Cake" of yellow cake and chocolate frosting and kicked it up a notch with a rich and fudgy chocolate sour cream frosting. Sprinkle with colored sugar for an extra festive look.

1 cup butter substitute, at room temperature

1½ cups evaporated cane juice

2 teapoons vanilla extract

3 cups unbleached flour

4 teaspoons baking powder

6 teaspoons egg replacer, whisked with 8 tablespoons warm water

1 cup soy milk

1 tablespoon white vinegar

CHOCOLATE SOUR CREAM FROSTING

2 cups gluten-free chocolate chips

½ cup butter substitute

2 teaspoons vanilla extract

¼ teaspoon salt

1⅓ cups tofu sour cream

7 cups organic powdered sugar

1. Preheat the oven to 350°F. Grease and flour two 9-inch round cake pans.

2. Using a stand mixer, beat the butter substitute, cane juice, and vanilla extract on medium speed until combined, about 20 seconds. Stop and scrape down the sides of the bowl, then increase the speed to high and whip the mixture until light and fluffy, about 2 minutes.

3. In a small bowl, mix the flour and baking powder. In a separate bowl, mix the egg replacer, soy milk, and vinegar. Alternate adding the dry and wet ingredients, starting and ending with the dry ingredients, and beat for 10 seconds after each addition. Stop and scrape down the sides of the bowl, making sure that all the butter is incorporated. Pour into the 2 prepared cake pans.

4. Bake the cake for 22 to 25 minutes, or until a toothpick inserted in the center of the cake comes out clean. Cool in the pans on wire racks for 10 minutes, then flip the pans over to release the cakes. Cool for another 30 minutes.

5. MEANWHILE, MAKE THE CHOCOLATE SOUR CREAM FROSTING: Melt the chocolate chips and butter substitute for 45 seconds in a microwave-safe bowl. Remove from the microwave and stir until the chocolate is completely melted and incorporated with the butter. Add the vanilla extract, salt, and sour cream, stirring until combined. Pour into a stand mixer and, with the motor running on medium speed, add the powdered sugar 2 cups at a time, until a desired consistency is reached.

6. When the cakes are cooled, place one layer on a serving dish. Using an offset spatula, spread a third of the frosting on top of the layer. Add the second layer and spread the remaining frosting on the sides and top of the cake.

CARROT CAKE

This carrot cake recipe came from my Aunt Maria. The secret ingredients are coconut and pineapple. The coconut lends a rich buttery flavor and the pineapple keeps the carrot cake supermoist.

2½ cups unbleached flour

2 cups evaporated cane juice

2 teaspoons baking powder

1 teaspoon baking soda

1 teaspoon salt

2½ teaspoons cinnamon

1 cup unsweetened coconut

1½ cups chopped walnuts, divided

1 cup vegetable oil

2 cups finely shredded carrots

½ cup raisins

8 ounces drained crushed pineapple

1 teaspoon vanilla extract

3 teaspoons egg replacer, whisked with 4 tablespoons warm water

CREAM CHEESE FROSTING

6 tablespoons butter substitute, at room temperature

8 ounces tofu cream cheese, at room temperature

1 teaspoon vanilla extract

4½ cups organic powdered sugar

1. Preheat the oven to 350°F. Grease and flour two 9-inch round baking pans.

2. Using a stand mixer, combine the flour, cane juice, baking powder, baking soda, salt, cinnamon, coconut, and ½ cup walnuts. Add the oil, carrots, raisins, pineapple, and vanilla extract. Mix for 30 seconds at medium speed. Stop and scrape down the sides of bowl. Add the egg replacer and mix for 30 more seconds.

3. Divide the batter into the two prepared baking pans and bake for 30 to 35 minutes, or until a toothpick inserted in the center of the cake comes out clean. Cool the pans on wire racks for 10 minutes, then flip the pans over to release cakes. Cool for another 45 minutes on the wire racks.

4. MEANWHILE, MAKE THE CREAM CHEESE FROSTING: In a stand mixer, beat the butter substitute, cream cheese, and vanilla extract until smooth. Scrape down sides of bowl and mix on medium speed for another 20 seconds. Decrease the speed to low and add the powdered sugar 1 cup at a time, stopping and scraping down the sides of the bowl after each addition. Once all the powdered sugar is combined, whip for one more 1 minute on high speed.

5. Place the first cake layer on a serving plate and spread with ¾ cup frosting in an even layer. Top with the second cake layer and spread the remaining cream cheese frosting on the top and sides of the cake. Garnish with the remaining 1 cup of walnuts around the sides of the cake. Keep refrigerated for up to 10 days.

RED VELVET CAKE

I make this moist and delicious cake vegan by using soy milk mixed with apple cider vinegar to make a "buttermilk," an essential ingredient in all red velvet cakes.

¾ cup butter substitute

2¼ cups evaporated cane juice

1 teaspoon salt

3 tablespoons cocoa powder

4½ teaspoons egg replacer, whisked with 6 tablespoons warm water

1½ cups soy milk

2 tablespoons plus 2 teaspoons white vinegar

2 teaspoons vanilla extract

3 tablespoons natural red food coloring

3¾ cups unbleached flour

2 teaspoons baking soda

Cream Cheese Frosting (page 66)

½ cup pecan halves, for finishing

1. Preheat the oven to 350°F. Grease and flour two 9-inch round baking pans.

2. Using a stand mixer, combine the butter substitute, cane juice, salt, and cocoa powder until light and fluffy, about 2 minutes at medium speed.

3. In a separate bowl, whisk the egg replacer with the soy milk, 2 tablespoons vinegar, vanilla extract, and red food coloring until well combined. With the stand mixer running, add the wet ingredients, alternating with the flour, into the mixer bowl, stopping and scraping down the sides and bottom of the bowl as needed, until all of the ingredients are well combined.

4. In a small bowl, mix the baking soda and 2 teaspoons vinegar. Fold into the batter. Divide the batter into the prepared baking pans and bake immediately for 25 to 30 minutes, or until a toothpick inserted in the center of the cake comes out clean. Cool in the pans on wire racks for 10 minutes, then flip the pans over to release the cakes. Cool another 45 minutes.

5. Place the first cake layer on a serving plate and spread with ¾ cup cream cheese frosting in an even layer. Top with the second cake layer and spread the remaining cream cheese frosting on the top and sides of the cake. Garnish with the pecan halves.

PUMPKIN SPICE CAKE

SERVES 12

This pumpkin spice cake is supermoist and flavorful. It will definitely beat out any non-vegan version. A sweet cream cheese frosting complements the spice of cinnamon and pumpkin.

1 cup unbleached flour

1 cup whole-wheat flour

1½ cups dark brown sugar

2 teaspoons baking powder

1 teaspoon baking soda

½ teaspoon salt

2 teaspoons cinnamon

¼ teaspoon pumpkin pie spice

½ cup vegetable oil

1 teaspoon vanilla extract

15 ounces pumpkin puree

½ cup soy milk

3 teaspoons egg replacer, whisked with 4 tablespoons warm water

Cream Cheese Frosting (page 66)

1. Preheat the oven to 350°F. Grease and flour a 9x13-inch baking pan.
2. Using a stand mixer, combine the flours, brown sugar, baking powder, baking soda, salt, cinnamon, and pumpkin pie spice. Add the oil, vanilla extract, pumpkin, and soy milk and mix on medium speed for 30 seconds. Stop and scrape down the sides of the bowl. Add the egg replacer and mix for another 30 seconds. Spread the batter into the prepared baking pan.
3. Bake for 25 to 30 minutes, or until a toothpick inserted in the center of the cake comes out clean. Cool in the pan on a wire rack for at least 1 hour. Invert the pan onto a serving platter and spread with the cream cheese frosting.

PUMPKIN CUPCAKES

MAKES 12 TO 14

For this recipe I took my moist yellow cake and added pumpkin puree, pumpkin pie spice, and cinnamon for a lightly pumpkin flavored cupcake. You can make these in standard-size cupcake liners or in minis, as shown in the photograph on page 2 of this book. They are delicious for breakfast, served with hot coffee or tea.

½ cup butter substitute

¾ cup evaporated cane juice

1 teaspoon vanilla extract

1½ cups unbleached flour

2 teaspoons baking powder

½ cup pumpkin puree

½ teaspoon pumpkin pie spice

½ teaspoon cinnamon

3 teaspoons egg replacer, whisked with 4 tablespoons warm water

½ cup soy milk

Cream Cheese Frosting (page 66)
Pumpkin pie spice, for sprinkling

1. Preheat the oven to 350°F. Line two standard-size 6-cavity muffin trays with paper liners.

2. Using a stand mixer, whip the butter substitute, cane juice, and vanilla extract until light and fluffy. Stop and scrape down the sides of the bowl. Add the flour, baking powder, pumpkin, pumpkin pie spice, and cinnamon. Mix for 30 seconds at low speed. Add the egg replacer and soy milk and beat for 30 seconds on medium speed. Pour ¼ cup of batter into each cupcake liner.

3. Bake for 15 to 18 minutes, or until a toothpick inserted in the center of a cupcake comes out clean. Cool in the baking trays on wire racks for 30 minutes before removing the cupcakes in their liners. Frost the cooled cupcakes with the cream cheese frosting, then sprinkle with pumpkin pie spice.

✳ *Gluten Free* ✳ RASPBERRY BUTTERCREAM CAKE

 **SERVES 8 TO 10**

Raspberry Buttercream Cake is a moist gluten-free cake perfect for a summer cookout. I love how the raspberries add a burst of flavor and color to the cake. Serve with raspberry iced tea and fresh mint.

CAKE

1 cup butter substitute, at room temperature

1½ cups evaporated cane juice

2 teaspoons vanilla extract

3 cups Gluten-Free Flour Mix (page 13)

4 teaspoons baking powder

6 teaspoons egg replacer, whisked with 8 tablespoons warm water

1 cup soy milk

1 tablespoon white vinegar

1 cup raspberries

BUTTERCREAM

1 cup butter substitute, at room temperature

3 cups organic powdered sugar

1 teaspoon vanilla extract

2 tablespoons water, optional

1. Preheat the oven to 350°F. Grease and flour three 9-inch baking pans.

2. FIRST MAKE THE CAKE: Using a stand mixer, beat the butter substitute, cane juice, and vanilla extract at medium speed until combined. Stop and scrape down the sides of the bowl, then turn the mixer to high speed and whip until light and fluffy, about 2 minutes.

3. Mix the flour and baking powder in a small bowl. In a separate bowl, mix the egg replacer, soy milk, and vinegar. Alternate adding the dry and wet ingredients to the mixer bowl, starting and ending with the dry ingredients. After each addition, beat for 10 seconds at low speed, then stop and scrape down the sides of the bowl, making sure that all the butter substitute is incorporated.

4. Cut the raspberries into quarters and gently fold into the batter. Pour the batter into the prepared baking pans.

5. Bake the cake for 22 to 25 minutes, or until a toothpick inserted in the center of the cake comes out clean. Cool the pans on wire racks for 10 minutes, then flip the pans over to release the cakes. Cool for another 30 minutes.

6. MEANWHILE, MAKE THE BUTTERCREAM: Using a stand mixer, beat the butter substitute until smooth. Stop and scrape down the sides and bottom of the bowl. Add the powdered sugar 1 cup at a time, mixing on low speed after each addition until well combined. Add the vanilla extract and whip for 1 minute at high speed. If the frosting is too thick to spread, add the water 1 tablespoon at a time. Whip an additional 2 minutes until light and fluffy.

COCONUT CAKE

Everyone needs a fantastic coconut cake recipe. A beautiful cake with tons of rich buttery coconut flavor, serve it outside on a hot summer day with freshly squeezed lemonade.

1 cup butter substitute, at room temperature

1½ cups evaporated cane juice

2 teaspoons vanilla extract

1 cup unsweetened coconut

3 cups unbleached flour

4 teaspoons baking powder

6 teaspoons egg replacer, whisked with 8 tablespoons warm water

1 cup soy milk

1 tablespoon white vinegar

COCONUT BUTTERCREAM

1 cup butter substitute, at room temperature

1 teaspoon vanilla extract

2 tablespoons water

3 cups organic powdered sugar

2 cups unsweetened coconut, for finishing

1. Preheat the oven to 350°F. Grease and flour three 9-inch round cake pans.

2. Using a stand mixer, beat the butter substitute, cane juice, vanilla extract, and coconut on medium speed until combined. Stop and scrape down the sides of the bowl, then increase the speed to high and whip the mixture until light and fluffy, about 2 minutes.

3. Mix the flour and baking powder in a small bowl. In a separate bowl, combine the egg replacer, soy milk, and vinegar. Alternate adding the dry and wet ingredients, starting and ending with the dry ingredients, to the mixer bowl. After each addition, beat at low speed for 10 seconds. Stop and scrape down the sides of the bowl, making sure that all the butter is incorporated. Pour into the prepared baking pans.

4. Bake the cake for 20 to 25 minutes, or until a toothpick inserted in the center of the cake comes out clean. Cool in the pans on wire racks for 10 minutes, then flip the pans over to release the cakes. Cool for another 45 minutes.

5. MEANWHILE, MAKE THE COCONUT BUTTERCREAM: Whip the butter substitute at medium speed until smooth, about 20 seconds. Stop and scrape down the sides of the bowl. Add the vanilla extract, water, and powdered sugar and mix for 30 seconds on low speed until combined, then whip for another 2 minutes at high speed until light and fluffy. Fold in ½ cup coconut.

6. When the cakes are cool, place the first layer onto a serving dish. Spread with ½ cup buttercream and top with ¼ cup coconut. Add the second cake layer and repeat. Add the third layer and spread the remaining buttercream on the top and sides of the cake. With your hand, press the remaining coconut to the sides and top of the cake.

PINEAPPLE UPSIDE-DOWN CAKE

Pineapple upside-down cake is one of my dad's favorite recipes. When you take the cake out of the oven and flip it over, the gooey brown sugar–pineapple topping drips down the sides of the moist yellow cake for a truly decadent experience. This is delicious served with your favorite non-dairy ice cream.

½ cup butter substitute

1 cup evaporated cane juice

1½ cups unbleached flour

2 teaspoons baking powder

½ teaspoon salt

¼ teaspoon cream of tartar

1 teaspoon vanilla extract

½ cup soy milk

3 teaspoons egg replacer, whisked with 4 tablespoons warm water

BROWN SUGAR PINEAPPLE TOPPING

4 tablespoons butter substitute, melted

¾ cup dark brown sugar

20-ounce can pineapple rings, drained

1. Preheat the oven to 350°F. Line the bottom of a 9-inch baking pan with greased parchment paper.

2. Using a stand mixer, whip the butter substitute and sugar until light and fluffy, about 2 minutes. Stop and scrape down the sides of the bowl. Add the flour, baking powder, salt, and cream of tartar. Mix for 30 seconds on medium speed. Add the vanilla extract, soy milk, and egg replacer and blend until combined. Set aside.

3. MAKE THE TOPPING: In a small bowl, combine the butter substitute and brown sugar. Spread it into the prepared baking pan. Place the pineapple rings onto the brown sugar mixture in one layer. Pour the cake batter on top and smooth with a spatula.

4. Bake the cake for 40 to 50 minutes, or until a toothpick inserted in the center of the cake comes out clean. Cool the pan on a wire rack for 10 minutes, then invert the pan onto a serving dish to release the cake. Cool for 45 more minutes before serving.

LEMON BUTTERCREAM CAKE

This refreshing cake has a great flavor combination of sweet and tart lemons with rich buttery coconut flakes. Garnish it with sliced lemons and lemon zest, and share this new recipe with friends.

1 cup butter substitute, at room temperature

1½ cups evaporated cane juice

2 teaspoons vanilla extract

3 cups unbleached flour

4 teapoons baking powder

6 teapoons egg replacer, whisked with 8 tablespoons warm water

1 cup soy milk

1 tablespoon white vinegar

1 teaspoon lemon extract

LEMON BUTTERCREAM

1 cup butter substitute, at room temperature

3 tablespoons fresh lemon juice

1 teaspoon vanilla extract

3 cups organic powdered sugar

TOPPING

2 cups unsweetened coconut

1 teaspoon lemon zest, for garnish

l lemon, thinly sliced into 8 slices, for garnish

1. Preheat the oven to 350°F. Grease and flour two 9-inch round cake pans.

2. Using a stand mixer, beat the butter substitute, cane juice, and vanilla extract on medium speed until combined, about 30 seconds. Stop and scrape down the sides of the bowl, then increase the speed to high and whip the batter until light and fluffy, about 5 minutes.

3. In a small bowl, mix the flour and baking powder. In a separate bowl, mix the egg replacer with the soy milk, vinegar, and lemon extract. Alternate adding the dry and wet ingredients, starting and ending with the dry ingredients, and beating for 10 seconds after each addition. Stop and scrape down the sides of the bowl, making sure that all the butter is incorporated. Pour into the prepared cake pans.

4. Bake for 20 to 25 minutes, or until a toothpick inserted in the center of the cake comes out clean. Cool in the pans on a wire rack for 10 minutes, then flip the pans over to release the cakes. Cool for another 45 minutes.

5. MEANWHILE, MAKE THE LEMON BUTTERCREAM: Beat the butter substitute on medium speed until smooth, about 20 seconds. Cut a lemon in half and juice 3 tablespoons. Add to the mixing bowl and mix for 30 seconds. Stop and scrape down the sides of the bowl. Add the vanilla extract and powdered sugar and mix for 30 seconds on low speed until well combined, then whip for 2 minutes until light and fluffy.

6. When the cakes are cooled, place one layer onto a serving dish. Using an offset spatula, spread with ¾ cup of the lemon buttercream and top with ½ cup coconut. Add the second cake layer and spread the remaining buttercream on the top and sides of the cake. Press the remaining coconut to the sides of the cake with your hand, and garnish with the lemon zest and lemon slices.

LEMON BUTTERCREAM CUPCAKES

 **MAKES 12 TO 15**

A derivative of the Lemon Buttercream Cake, these moist and flavorful cupcakes are great for a picnic, party, or just a treat after work. The slightly tart buttercream gives a burst of flavor to the sweet lemony cupcake. Sprinkle the lemon zest garnish on top for a pop of color.

1 cup butter substitute, at room temperature

1½ cups evaporated cane juice

2 teaspoons vanilla extract

3 teapoons lemon extract

1 tablespoon lemon zest, plus more for garnish

3 cups unbleached flour

4 teaspoons baking powder

6 teaspoons egg replacer, whisked with 8 tablespoons warm water

1 cup soy milk

1 tablespoon white vinegar

Lemon Buttercream (page 77)

1 teaspoon lemon zest, for garnish

1. Preheat the oven to 350°F. Line 15 standard-size cupcake cavities with paper liners.

2. Using a stand mixer, beat the butter substitute, cane juice, vanilla extract, lemon extract, and lemon zest until combined. Stop and scrape down the sides and bottom of the bowl, then increase the speed to high and whip the mixture until light and fluffy, about 2 minutes.

3. In a medium bowl, mix the flour and baking powder. In a separate bowl, combine the egg replacer, soy milk, and vinegar. Alternate adding the dry and wet ingredients, starting and ending with the dry ingredients, and beat for 10 seconds after each addition. Stop and scrape down the sides of the bowl, making sure that all the butter is incorporated. Then beat for 30 more seconds on medium speed. Spoon the batter a quarter way up each cupcake liner.

4. Bake for 20 to 25 minutes, or until a toothpick inserted in the center comes out clean. Cool in the pans on wire racks for 10 minutes, then take out the cupcakes and cool for another 20 minutes. Ice the top of each cupcake with the lemon buttercream and garnish with lemon zest and a lemon slice.

Gluten-Free CRANBERRY ORANGE BUNDT CAKE

 **SERVES 10 TO 12**

Moist and gluten-free are not usually in the same sentence but this bundt cake is very moist indeed. The unique flavor combinations of cranberry and pumpkin spice mixed with pecan and orange add a depth of flavor unlike anything you have tried before. And it's so delicious when drizzled with an orange juice–sugar glaze.

2½ cups Gluten-Free Flour Mix (page 13)

1 teaspoon baking powder

½ teaspoon baking soda

1 teaspoon salt

1 tablespoon pumpkin pie spice

½ cup butter substitute

½ cup evaporated cane juice

¼ teaspoon orange zest

1½ cups unsweetened applesauce

3 teaspoons egg replacer, whisked with 4 tablespoons warm water

½ cup chopped pecans

1 cup organic dried cranberries

ORANGE GLAZE

1 cup organic powdered sugar

2 tablespoons orange juice

1. Preheat the oven to 350°F. Grease and flour a bundt pan.

2. In a large bowl, combine the flour, baking powder, baking soda, salt, and pumpkin pie spice. Set aside.

3. Using a stand mixer, beat the butter substitute, cane juice, and orange zest on high speed until light and fluffy, about 2 minutes. Stop and scrape down the sides of the bowl and add the applesauce, flour mixture, egg replacer, pecans, and cranberries. Mix for 30 seconds on high speed. Pour the batter into the prepared bundt pan.

4. Bake the cake for 50 to 60 minutes, or until a toothpick inserted in the center comes out clean. Cool in the pan on a wire rack for 10 minutes, then invert the pan to release the cake. Cool for 1 hour.

5. Meanwhile, in a small bowl, whisk the powdered sugar and orange juice until combined. Pour over the cooled cake before serving.

CHOCOLATE GANACHE CAKE

 **SERVES 8 TO 10**

My stepmom learned this recipe from her mom, and passed it on to me when I was in middle school. The coffee brings out the rich chocolate flavor. One of my all-time bestsellers.

CHOCOLATE CAKE

1¾ cups unbleached flour

2 cups evaporated cane juice

¾ cup cocoa powder

1 teaspoon baking powder

2 teaspoons baking soda

1 teaspoon salt

1 cup strong coffee, cooled

½ cup vegetable oil

1 teaspoon pure vanilla extract

1 cup soy milk and white vinegar*

3 teaspoons egg replacer, whisked with 4 tablespoons warm water

CHOCOLATE BUTTERCREAM

1 cup butter substitute, softened

3 cups organic powdered sugar

¼ cup cocoa powder

2 tablespoons water

CHOCOLATE GANACHE

1 cup gluten-free chocolate chips

6 tablespoons butter substitute

*Pour 1 tablespoon white vinegar into a measuring cup, then add the soy milk to equal 1 cup

1. Preheat the oven to 350°F. Grease and flour two 9-inch round cake pans.

2. In a stand mixer, place the flour, cane juice, cocoa powder, baking powder, baking soda, and salt and stir to combine.

3. In a separate bowl, whisk the cooled coffee, oil, vanilla extract, and soy milk/vinegar mixture. Turn the stand mixer to low speed, and slowly pour the liquid mixture into the dry ingredients. Mix for 1 minute. Stop and scrape down the sides and bottom of the bowl. Add the egg replacer and mix again for 1 minute at medium speed. The cake batter will be very thin. Divide it between the prepared cake pans.

4. Bake for 25 to 30 minutes, or until a toothpick inserted in the center of the cake comes out clean. Cool the pans on wire racks for 10 minutes, then flip the pans over to release the cakes. Cool for 1 hour.

5. MEANWHILE, MAKE THE CHOCOLATE BUTTERCREAM: Using a stand mixer, beat the butter substitute on medium speed until smooth in texture, about 20 seconds. Stop and scrape down the sides of the bowl. Add the powdered sugar and cocoa powder and mix for 1 minute on low speed. Add the water and mix on medium speed until combined, then increase the speed to high for 2 minutes, until the buttercream is light and fluffy. Set aside.

6. MAKE THE CHOCOLATE GANACHE: In a microwave-safe bowl, melt the chocolate chips and butter substitute on 75 percent power for 45 seconds. Remove from the microwave and stir until the chocolate is completely melted. Set aside.

7. When the cake is cooled, place the first layer on a serving plate. Spread 1 cup of chocolate buttercream on top. Place the second layer on top and spread the remaining buttercream on the top and sides of the cake. Pour the ganache on top of the frosted cake and spread it over the sides of cake with an offset spatula.

GERMAN CHOCOLATE CAKE

The homemade caramel, coconut, and pecan frosting in this recipe is to die for. Be careful if you make this with company—you may not get the frosting on to the cake before it's polished off in the bowl! I guarantee that everyone will want your recipe and no one will be able to tell it's vegan.

1¾ cups unbleached flour

2 cups evaporated cane juice

¾ cup cocoa powder

1 teaspoon baking powder

2 teaspoons baking soda

1 teapoon salt

1 cup strong coffee, cooled

½ cup vegetable oil

1 teaspoon vanilla extract

1 cup soy milk and white vinegar*

3 teaspoons egg replacer, whisked with 4 tablespoons warm water

GERMAN CHOCOLATE FROSTING

½ cup butter substitute

½ cup soy milk

1½ cups unsweetened coconut

1 cup chopped pecans

½ cup evaporated cane juice

1 teaspoon vanilla extract

Chocolate Buttercream (page 82)

*Pour 1 tablespoon white vinegar into a measuring cup, then add the soy milk to equal 1 cup.

1. Preheat the oven to 350°F. Grease and flour two 9-inch round cake pans.

2. In a stand mixer, combine the flour, cane juice, cocoa powder, baking powder, baking soda, and salt. Stir to combine.

3. In a separate bowl, whisk the coffee, oil, vanilla extract, and soy milk/vinegar mixture. Turn the mixer to low speed and slowly pour the liquid mixture into the dry ingredients. Mix for 1 minute. Stop and scrape down the sides and bottom of the bowl. Add the egg replacer and mix again for 1 minute. The cake batter will be very thin. Divide it between the prepared cake pans.

4. Bake for 25 to 30 minutes, or until a toothpick inserted in the center of the cake comes out clean. Cool in the pans on wire racks for 10 minutes, then flip the pans over to release the cakes. Cool for 1 hour.

5. Meanwhile, make the German chocolate frosting: In a saucepan, melt the butter substitute. Add the soy milk, coconut, pecans, cane juice, and vanilla extract. Stir until combined, then heat for 2 minutes or until the mixture comes to a boil.

6. When the cakes have cooled, place the first layer on a serving plate. Using an offset spatula, spread half of the German chocolate frosting on top, then add the second layer of cake, and spread the remaining German chocolate frosting on top of that. Frost the sides of the cake with the chocolate buttercream.

✳ *Gluten-Free* ✳
CHOCOLATE CUPCAKES

MAKES 24

Here I took my famous chocolate cake recipe and used my gluten-free flour mix in place of all-purpose flour. Moist and delicious as ever, you will not be able to tell these cupcakes are gluten-free.

1¾ cups Gluten Free Flour Mix (page 13)

2 cups evaporated cane juice

¾ cup cocoa powder

1 teaspoon baking powder

2 teapoons baking soda

1 teaspoon salt

1 cup strong coffee, cooled

½ cup vegetable oil

1 teaspoon vanilla extract

1 cup soy milk and white vinegar*

3 teaspoons egg replacer, whisked with 4 tablespoons warm water

Coconut Buttercream (page 75, but decrease unsweetened coconut to 1½ cups)

Chocolate Buttercream (page 82)

*Pour 1 tablespoon white vinegar into a measuring cup, and add soy milk to equal 1 cup.

1. Preheat the oven to 350°F. Line 24 cupcake cavities with paper liners

2. In a stand mixer, combine the flour, cane juice, cocoa powder, baking powder, baking soda, and salt. In a separate bowl, whisk the coffee, oil, vanilla extract, and soy milk/vinegar mixture. Turn the mixer to medium speed and slowly pour the liquid mixture into the dry ingredients. Mix for 1 minute. Add the egg replacer and mix again for 1 minute. The batter will be thin. Pour ¼ cup of the batter into each cupcake liner.

3. Bake for 18 to 20 minutes, or until a toothpick inserted in the center of a cupcake comes out clean. Cool on wire racks for 30 minutes.

4. MEANWHILE, MAKE THE COCONUT BUTTERCREAM: Using a stand mixer, beat the butter substitute until smooth in texture. Stop and scrape down the sides of the bowl and add the powdered sugar. Mix for 1 minute on low speed. Add ¾ cup coconut, the water, and vanilla extract. Mix on high speed for 30 seconds, or until combined and fluffy.

5. Frost half of the cooled cupcakes with the coconut buttercream and top with the remaining coconut. Frost the other half of the cooled cupcakes with the chocolate buttercream.

BLACK BOTTOMS

Black Bottoms are a classic dessert that my relatives always had at family gatherings. They are a real crowd pleaser and, with these vegan and gluten-free variations, now everyone can enjoy these fun-looking sweet cupcakes.

CHOCOLATE CAKE

1½ cups unbleached flour or Gluten-Free Flour Mix (page 13)

1 cup evaporated cane juice

1 teaspoon baking soda

¼ cup cocoa powder

1 cup water

⅓ cup vegetable oil

1 teaspoon vanilla extract

1 tablespoon white vinegar

CREAM CHEESE TOPPING

8 ounces tofu cream cheese, at room temperature

⅓ cup evaporated cane juice

¼ teaspoon salt

1½ teaspoons egg replacer, whisked with 1 tablespoon warm water

1 cup gluten-free chocolate chips

1. Preheat the oven to 350°F. Fill 14 standard-sized muffin cavities with cupcake liners.

2. MAKE THE CHOCOLATE CAKE: In a medium bowl, mix the flour, cane juice, baking soda, and cocoa powder. Pour in the water, oil, vanilla extract, and vinegar. Stir until combined. Pour ¼ cup into each cupcake liner. Set aside.

3. NEXT MAKE THE CREAM CHEESE TOPPING: Using a stand mixer, beat the cream cheese until smooth. Add the cane juice and salt. Mix for 30 seconds then stop and scrape down the sides of the bowl. Add the egg replacer and blend on medium speed for 30 seconds. Stir in the chocolate chips. Spoon 2 tablespoons of the mixture on top of each chocolate bottom.

4. Bake the black bottoms for 18 to 22 minutes, or until a toothpick inserted in the center comes out clean. Cool on wire racks. Refrigerate the cupcakes for up to 14 days. These can also be frozen for up to 3 months in an airtight container.

PB&J CUPCAKES

PB&J was my favorite sandwich growing up, so I decided to make it into a cupcake. Yellow cake is used for two slices of bread, strawberry jam is sandwiched in between, and a rich peanut butter buttercream ties it all together. If only I could have had these in my lunchbox when I was in school!

1 cup butter substitute

1½ cups evaporated cane juice

2 teaspoons vanilla extract

3 cups unbleached flour

4 teaspoons baking powder

6 teaspoons egg replacer, whisked with 8 tablespoons warm water

1 cup soy milk

PEANUT BUTTER BUTTERCREAM

½ cup unsweetened peanut butter

1 cup butter substitute, softened

3 cups organic powdered sugar

1 tablespoon soy milk

1 teaspoon vanilla extract

12 ounces strawberry jam

1. Preheat the oven to 350°F. Line 18 standard-size muffin cavities with cupcake liners.

2. Using a stand mixer, beat the butter substitute, cane juice, and vanilla extract on medium speed until light and fluffy, about 3 minutes. Stop and scrape down the sides of the bowl.

3. Sift the flour and baking powder together in a small bowl and set aside. In a separate bowl, mix the egg replacer and soy milk. With the motor running at low speed, alternate adding the dry ingredients and wet ingredients, beginning and ending with the dry ingredients. Beat for 30 seconds on medium speed. Stop and scrape down the sides and bottom of the bowl and mix for 30 more seconds on medium speed. Pour ¼ cup batter into each cupcake liner.

4. Bake the cupcakes for 18 to 20 minutes, or until a toothpick inserted in the center of a cupcake comes out clean. Cool on wire racks for about 30 minutes before removing cupcakes.

5. MEANWHILE, MAKE THE PEANUT BUTTER BUTTERCREAM: Using a stand mixer, beat the butter substitute on medium speed until smooth, about 30 seconds. Stop and scrape down the sides of the bowl. Add the peanut butter and mix for 30 seconds. Add the powdered sugar, soy milk, and vanilla extract and mix on low speed until the powdered sugar is incorporated, then mix on high speed for 1 minute until fluffy. Set aside.

6. When the cupcakes are cool, unwrap each cupcake and cut it in half. Spoon 1 tablespoon of strawberry jam onto the bottom half of each cupcake. Frost the top half of each cupcake with peanut butter buttercream, then sandwich the two halves together, with the jam on bottom.

STRAWBERRY LEMON CUPCAKES

MAKES 20

A fun recipe to make with your family, the strawberry buttercream bursts from these cupcakes and the lemon glaze drips down the sides. Definitely have plenty of napkins on hand when serving.

1 cup butter substitute, at room temperature

1½ cups evaporated cane juice

2 teaspoons vanilla extract

3 cups unbleached flour

4 teaspoons baking powder

6 teapoons egg replacer, whisked with 8 tablespoons warm water

1 cup soy milk

1 tablespoon white vinegar

STRAWBERRY BUTTERCREAM

1 cup butter substitute, at room temperature

¼ cup plus 3 tablespoons strawberries

3½ cups organic powdered sugar

LEMON GLAZE

1 cup powdered sugar

1 tablespoon lemon juice

1 tablespoon water

1. Preheat the oven to 350°F. Fill 20 standard-size cupcake cavities with paper liners.

2. Using a stand mixer, beat the butter substitute, cane juice, and vanilla extract on medium speed until combined, about 20 seconds. Stop and scrape down the sides of the bowl, then increase the speed to high and whip the mixture until light and fluffy, about 2 minutes.

3. In a small bowl, mix the flour and baking powder. In a separate bowl, mix the egg replacer, soy milk, and vinegar. Alternate adding the dry and wet ingredients, starting and ending with the dry ingredients, and beating for 10 seconds after each addition. Stop and scrape down the sides of the bowl, making sure that all the butter is incorporated. Fill each cupcake liner with ¼ cup batter.

4. Bake for 20 to 25 minutes, or until a toothpick inserted in the center of a cupcake comes out clean. Take the cupcakes out of the baking trays and cool on wire racks for 30 minutes.

5. MEANWHILE, MAKE THE STRAWBERRY BUTTERCREAM: In a stand mixer, whip the butter substitute on medium speed until smooth, about 30 seconds. In a food processor or blender, puree the strawberries. Add to the mixer bowl and mix for 30 seconds. Stop and scrape down the sides of the bowl. Add the powdered sugar and mix for 30 seconds on low speed, until powdered sugar is combined. Whip the buttercream for another 2 minutes until light and fluffy. Set aside.

6. MAKE THE LEMON GLAZE: In a small bowl, whisk the powdered sugar, lemon juice, and water. Set aside.

7. When the cupcakes are cool, spoon the strawberry buttercream into a piping bag or zip-top bag, with the bottom corner cut. Squeeze the buttercream into the top of each cupcake until the cupcake starts to split open. Drizzle with the lemon glaze.

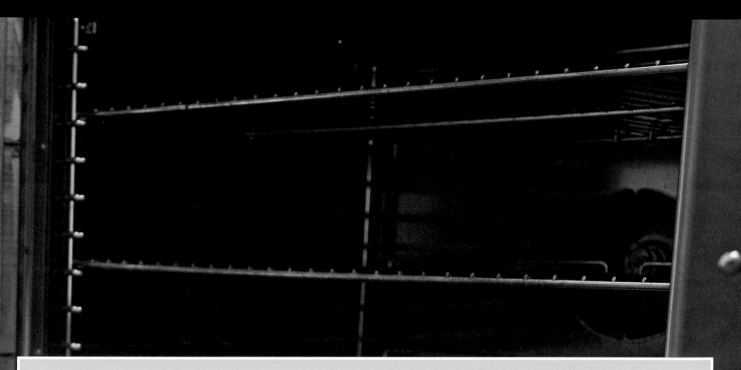

✴ Cookies, Brownies, ✴ and Bars

✳ RECIPE LIST ✳

Gluten-Free ✴
ALMOND JAM COOKIES

 MAKES 9 TO 12

These delicious gluten-free cookies have a nutty almond flavor combined with sweet strawberry jam. An old family recipe, these are great with a glass of peach iced tea.

½ cup butter substitute

¼ cup evaporated cane juice

1 teaspoon vanilla extract

¼ teaspoon almond extract

1 cup Gluten-Free Flour Mix (page 13)

¼ teaspoon salt

1½ teaspoons egg replacer, whisked with 2 tablespoons warm water

½ cup finely chopped almonds

½ cup organic strawberry jam

1. Preheat the oven to 350°F. Line two cookies sheets with aluminum foil or parchment paper.

2. Using a stand mixer, cream the butter substitute and cane juice until light and fluffy. Add the vanilla and almond extracts, mixing until combined. Stop the machine and scrape down the sides and bottom of the bowl. Then add the flour and salt. Mix on medium speed for 30 seconds. Stop and scrape down the sides of bowl again. Add the egg replacer and mix for 30 seconds, until a ball of dough forms. Wrap the cookie dough in plastic wrap and refrigerate for 1 hour.

3. Once the dough is chilled, roll it into 1-inch balls, flouring your hands as necessary. Spread the chopped almonds on a baking sheet, then roll the balls through them to cover on all sides. Press your thumb into the center of each ball, fill with ½ teaspoon of jam, and place on the prepared cookie sheets.

4. Bake the cookies for 12 to 14 minutes or until they have browned. Place on wire racks to cool. Store in an airtight container.

ALMOND SNICKERDOODLES

 **MAKES 12 TO 15**

This recipe gives the classic Christmas-time cinnamon sugar snickerdoodle cookie a twist with pure almond extract. The almond adds another level of unexpected flavor. These are best served warm right out the oven.

1 cup butter substitute

1½ cups plus 2 tablespoons evaporated cane juice

3 cups flour

1 teaspoon baking soda

½ teaspoon salt

1 teaspoon cream of tartar

3 teaspoons egg replacer, whisked with 4 tablespoons warm water

1 teaspoon vanilla extract

1 teaspoon almond extract

2 teaspoons cinnamon

1. Preheat the oven to 400°F. Line two cookies sheets with aluminum foil or parchment paper.

2. Using a stand mixer, beat the butter substitute and 1½ cups cane juice on medium speed until light and fluffy, about 2 minutes. Stop the machine and scrape down the sides of the bowl. Add the flour, baking soda, salt, and cream of tartar and mix at medium speed for 1 minute. Stop and scrape down the sides of the bowl again. Add the egg replacer and vanilla and almond extracts. Beat on medium speed until combined, around 30 seconds, until a ball of dough forms.

3. Remove the dough and roll into 1-inch balls, flouring your hands as necessary.

4. In a separate small bowl, combine the 2 tablespoons cane juice with the cinnamon. Roll the cookie dough balls into mixture to cover all around, then lightly press the tongs of a fork into the cookies.

5. Bake the cookies on the prepared cookie sheets for 8 to 10 minutes, or until golden brown. Store in an airtight container for up to a week.

PECAN SHORTBREAD COOKIES

Known by many names, such as Mexican Wedding Cookies, Russian Tea Cookies, or Snowman Cookies, these treats are loved by all. This vegan version doesn't miss a step. Just delicious.

1 cup butter substitute

1 cup evaporated cane juice

2 cups unbleached flour

¼ teaspoon salt

1½ cups finely chopped pecans

2 teaspoons vanilla extract

½ cup organic powdered sugar

1. Preheat the oven to 350°F. Line two baking sheets with aluminum foil or parchment paper.

2. Using a stand mixer, whip the butter substitute and cane juice on high speed until light and fluffy, about 2 minutes. Stop and scrape down the sides of the bowl. Add the flour, salt, pecans, and vanilla extract. Mix for 30 seconds. If the dough is too soft to roll, cover with plastic wrap and refrigerate for 1 hour.

3. Roll the dough into 1-inch balls, flouring your hands as necessary, and place on the prepared cookie sheets.

4. Bake the cookies for 10 to 12 minutes. Cool on wire racks. Once cooled, roll in the powdered sugar. Store in an airtight container at room temperature, or freeze, in an airtight container or freezer bag, for up to 3 months.

CHOCOLATE GRAHAM CRACKERS

 MAKES 30

Delicious on their own but also great when making pie crusts, these graham crackers have all-natural ingredients and don't have the high-fructose corn syrup like store brands.

½ cup unbleached flour

1½ cups whole-wheat flour

½ cup evaporated cane juice, divided

½ cup cocoa powder

½ teaspoon salt

1 teaspoon baking powder

4 tablespoons butter substitute

2 tablespoons light agave

1 tablespoon molasses

¼ cup water

1. Preheat the oven to 350°F. Line two cookie sheets with aluminum foil or parchment paper.

2. Using a stand mixer, combine the flours, cane juice, cocoa powder, salt, and baking powder. With the motor running at medium speed, add the butter substitute 1 tablespoon at a time, waiting 10 seconds after each addition. Continue blending until the mixture resembles coarse sand, about 1 minute.

3. In a small bowl, combine the agave, molasses, and water. Add to the flour mixture and blend until it forms a ball, about 1 minute. Wrap in plastic wrap and chill for 1 hour in the refrigerator.

4. Lightly flour your work surface, rolling pin, and the chilled dough. Roll it out as thin as possible. Using a knife, cut the dough into squares, or use any shaped cookie cutter. Place the crackers on the prepared baking sheets, about 1 inch apart. Prick with a fork and lightly brush each cracker with water and sprinkle with the remaining ½ cup cane juice.

5. Bake for 13 to 15 minutes until the crackers are crisp. Store in an airtight container for up to 2 weeks.

AGAVE GRAHAM CRACKERS

Agave gives this vegan version of a honey graham cracker the sweet flavor that honey does without actually using honey. This cracker is a staple for recipes like s'mores, as seen on the next page.

½ cup unbleached flour

2 cups whole-wheat flour

½ cup evaporated cane juice, divided

½ teaspoon salt

1 teaspoon baking powder

1 teaspoon cinnamon

4 tablespoons butter substitute

2 tablespoons light agave

1 tablespoon molasses

¼ cup water

1. Preheat the oven to 350°F. Line two baking sheets with aluminum foil or parchment paper.

2. Using a stand mixer, combine the flours, ¼ cup cane juice, salt, baking powder, and cinnamon. With the motor running on medium speed, add the butter substitute 1 tablespoon at a time, waiting 10 seconds after each addition. Continue blending until the mixture resembles coarse sand, about 1 minute.

3. In a small bowl, combine the agave, molasses, and water. Add to the flour mixture and blend on medium speed until it forms a ball. Wrap it in plastic wrap and chill for 1 hour in the refrigerator.

4. After dough has chilled, Lightly flour your work surface, a rolling pin, and the ball of dough. Roll it out as thin as possible. Using a knife, cut the dough into squares, or use any shaped cookie cutter. Place the crackers on the prepared baking sheets, about 1 inch apart. Prick with a fork. Lightly brush each cracker with water and sprinkle with the remaining ¼ cup cane juice.

5. Bake for 13 to 15 minutes until the crackers are crisp. Store in an airtight container for up to 2 weeks.

S'MORES

MAKES 8

Who doesn't love s'mores? In this recipe I use Sweet & Sara brand marshmallows. They toast just like non-vegan marshmalllows and taste a lot better too. Have enough at your next bonfire with friends.

16 Agave Graham Crackers
(see opposite)
16 vegan marshmallows
1 cup gluten-free chocolate chips

1. Preheat the oven to 375°F. Line a baking sheet with aluminum foil.
2. Place 8 graham crackers onto the prepared baking sheet. Top each cracker with 2 marshmallows. Heat in the oven for 8 minutes, or until the marshmallows begin to brown and fluff.
3. Meanwhile, in a microwave-safe bowl, melt the chocolate chips on 75 percent power for 2 minutes, stirring after each 30-second interval. Remove from the microwave and stir the chocolate until it is completely melted.
4. Spoon the melted chocolate on the remaining 8 graham crackers. Sandwich the marshmallow-topped crackers and chocolate crackers together. Serve immediately.

* Raw *
CINNAMON RAISIN COOKIES

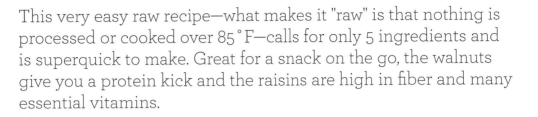

MAKES 16

This very easy raw recipe—what makes it "raw" is that nothing is processed or cooked over 85°F—calls for only 5 ingredients and is superquick to make. Great for a snack on the go, the walnuts give you a protein kick and the raisins are high in fiber and many essential vitamins.

1 cup raw walnuts

2 cups raisins

1¾ cups unsweetened coconut

1 teaspoon cinnamon

2 teaspoons coconut oil

1. Using a food processor, blend the walnuts until finely ground. Pour into a separate bowl.

2. Blend the raisins in the food processor for 4 minutes on high speed, until they turn into a paste, stopping and scraping down the sides of the bowl as necessary. Add the walnuts, 1¼ cups coconut, cinnamon, and coconut oil. Process on high speed for 3 minutes, or until all the ingredients come together.

3. Form into sixteen 2½-inch cookies and press the remaining ½ cup coconut on both sides of the cookies. Store in the refrigerator for up to 3 days.

PEANUT BUTTER BROWNIES

 **MAKES 12 TO 15**

The vegan brownie seems to be one of the hardest to master as most come out too cake-like. But my recipe comes out moist and chewy. Adding peanut butter and a chocolate drizzle make these brownies an indulgent treat. These are great treats for a picnic or cookout, or just served with a glass of your favorite non-dairy milk.

2 cups unbleached flour

2 cups evaporated cane juice

¾ cup cocoa powder

1 teaspoon baking powder

1 teaspoon salt

1 cup water

1 cup vegetable oil

1½ teaspoons vanilla extract

¼ cup natural unsweetened peanut butter

½ cup melted gluten-free chocolate chips

1. Preheat the oven to 350°F. Line and grease a 9 x 13-inch baking pan with aluminum foil or parchment paper.

2. Using a stand mixer, combine the flour, cane juice, cocoa powder, baking powder, and salt. Add the water, oil, and vanilla extract and mix on medium speed for 1 minute, until combined. Pour into the prepared baking pan.

3. Spoon the peanut butter onto each corner and the center of the brownie batter. Using a dull knife, swirl the peanut butter into the brownie batter to create a marbled effect.

4. Bake for 20 to 25 minutes. Cool the pan on a wire rack for 30 minutes, then invert the pan on a cutting board and peel away the parchment or foil. Cut into brownies and drizzle with the melted chocolate.

CRÈME DE MENTHE BROWNIES

These brownies were one of my favorite desserts when I was a kid. My Aunt Trisha made them for special occasions and I would anxiously wait for dinner to be over so I could indulge. The moist brownie, cool mint filling, and chocolate ganache topping are one of the most delicious combinations you will ever taste.

BROWNIE

2 cups unbleached flour

2 cups evaporated cane juice

¾ cup cocoa powder

1 teaspoon baking powder

1 teaspoon salt

1 cup water

1 cup vegetable oil

1½ teaspoons vanilla

CRÈME DE MENTHE FILLING

½ cup butter substitute at room temperature

2 cups organic powdered sugar

4 tablespoons Crème de Menthe liquor

CHOCOLATE GANACHE

1 cup gluten-free chocolate chips

6 tablespoons butter substitute

1. Preheat the oven to 350°F. Grease and lightly flour a 9 x 13-inch baking pan.

2. FIRST MAKE THE BROWNIES: Using a stand mixer, combine the flour, cane juice, cocoa powder, baking powder, and salt. Add the water, vegetable oil, and vanilla extract and blend on medium speed for 1 minute, or until well combined. Pour into the prepared baking pan. Bake for 20 to 25 minutes, then cool in the pan on a wire rack for 1 hour.

3. MEANWHILE, MAKE CRÈME DE MENTHE FILLING: Using a stand mixer, whip the butter substitute until smooth. Stop and scrape down the sides of the bowl. Add the powdered sugar and liquor and blend for 1 minute. Spread evenly on the cooled brownie cake.

4. To make the Chocolate Ganache, melt the chocolate chips and butter substitute in a microwave-safe bowl for 1 minute in the microwave. Stir until completely melted and pour over the crème de menthe filling. Spread evenly with an offset spatula. Cover with plastic wrap and place in the freezer immediately to set, about 10 minutes.

5. Cut the chilled mixture into brownies with a sharp knife*. Store in an airtight container in the refrigerator for up to 14 days, or in the freezer for up to 3 months.

*For easier cutting, warm the knife under hot water, dry it, and cut the brownies. This will also allow the brownies to have clean edges.

MARSHMALLOW BARS

I think every kid in America has had a "Rice Krispies Treat" at some point in their lives. So this is a throwback to childhood. I use Dandies brand marshmallows for these and they taste exactly how you remember. These bars are also really good dipped in chocolate or peanut butter. Yum!

3 tablespoons butter substitute

4 cups vegan marshmallows

6 cups organic rice cereal

1. In a large pot, melt the butter substitute over medium heat. Once melted, add the marshmallows and stir until completely melted, about 5 minutes. Turn the heat off and stir in the cereal.

2. Line the bottom of a 9 x 13-inch baking pan with parchment paper. Grease the paper and the sides of the pan really well. Pour the marshmallow mixture into the pan and press into the shape of the pan with a greased spatula.

3. Let cool for 10 minutes before cutting into bars. Store in an airtight container for up to a week.

❋ Raw ❋
CASHEW CAROB BARS

 MAKES 14

Another raw recipe that is so quick and easy—all you need is a food processor for these delicious power bars. Great for snacking or while on a hike or biking a wooded trail.

1 cup raw cashews, plus 12 for garnish

2 cups dried dates

¼ cup carob chips

2 teaspoons coconut oil

1 teaspoon lemon juice

3 teaspoons light agave

1 cup shredded unsweetened coconut

1. Using a food processor, blend the 1 cup of cashews until finely ground. Pour into a separate bowl and set aside.

2. Blend the dates, carob chips, coconut oil, lemon juice, agave, and coconut for 4 minutes on high speed. Stop and scrape down the sides of the bowl as needed. Add the reserved cashews and blend again for 2 minutes, or until the ingredients form a paste.

3. Shape into 3-inch bars and place a whole cashew on top of each for garnish. Store in the refrigerator for up to 3 days.

RASPBERRY CHOCOLATE BARS

MAKES 12 TO 15

This is my version of a kicked-up linzer cookie. The addition of chocolate and pecans adds a rich depth of flavor to a deliciously sweet raspberry jam cookie. I also love the addition of oats.

1½ cups unbleached flour

1 cup dark brown sugar

1 teaspoon baking powder

1 cup butter substitute

1½ cups quick oats

½ cup unsweetened coconut

½ cup chopped pecans

12 ounces raspberry jam

½ cup gluten-free chocolate chips

1. Preheat the oven to 350°F. Grease and flour an 8 x 8-inch baking pan.

2. Using a stand mixer, combine the flour, brown sugar, and baking powder at medium speed. With the motor still running, add the butter substitute in tablespoons every 10 seconds until the batter resembles coarse sand. Add the oats, coconut, and pecans. Press one third of the dough into the prepared baking pan. Spoon the jam on top of the dough and sprinkle with the chocolate chips. Place the remaining dough on top.

3. Bake for 25 to 30 minutes, until bubbly and golden brown. Cool in the baking pan on a wire rack for 30 minutes, then cut the bars into triangles in the pan and serve.

CHOCOLATE PEANUT BUTTER BARS

Here is my vegan—and healthier—version of a peanut butter cup.
Not only is it delicious, but it's no-bake, so it's quick and easy too!

PEANUT LAYER

2 cups organic powdered sugar

1½ cups finely crushed agave graham crackers (about 14), page 104

1 cup natural peanut butter

½ cup butter substitute, at room temperature

3 tablespoons water

CHOCOLATE LAYER

1 cup gluten-free chocolate chips

6 tablespoons butter substitute

1. FIRST MAKE THE PEANUT LAYER: Using a stand mixer, combine the powdered sugar and crushed graham crackers. Add the peanut butter, butter substitute, and water and blend for 1 minute on medium speed. The mixture will be very thick. Press it into a foil-lined, 8 x 8-inch square pan and set aside.

2. NEXT MAKE THE CHOCOLATE LAYER: In a microwave-safe bowl, combine the chocolate chips and butter substitute. Melt for 30 to 45 seconds, checking to make sure the chocolate doesn't melt completely. Remove from the microwave and stir the chocolate mixture until it is completely melted.

3. Spoon the chocolate layer on top of the peanut layer and spread evenly. Chill in the refrigerator for 1 hour before cutting into 2x2-inch squares.

✳ Everything Sweet ✳
In Between

✳ RECIPE LIST ✳

Gluten-Free ✳
BAKED APPLES

 SERVES 4

This is one of my new favorites. For this filling, you can mix any dried fruit combinations you like: cherries and apricots, peaches and raisins, strawberries and blueberries, the possibilities are endless. These are great served warm right out of the oven.

4 large firm apples

¼ cup dark brown sugar

1 teaspoon cinnamon

¼ cup golden raisins

¼ cup cranberries

¼ cup chopped pecans

1 tablespoon butter substitute

¾ cup water

1. Preheat the oven to 375°F.

2. Wash and dry the apples. Using a melon baller, remove the core of the apples to ½ inch from the bottom. Make a hole at the top of each apple 1 inch wide.

3. In a mixing bowl, combine the brown sugar, cinnamon, raisins, cranberries, and pecans. Stuff each apple with a quarter of the mixture. Top each apple with 1 tablespoon of the butter substitute. Place the apples in an 8x8-inch square pan.

4. In a microwave-safe bowl, heat the water for 1 minute or until the water boils. Pour the boiling water into the pan around the apples. Bake for 30 to 40 minutes, or until the apples are tender but not mushy. Baking time will depend on how large the apples are.

Raw
MELON SOUP

 SERVES 4

What a cute way to get our fruit servings for the day. A super simple recipe with only 4 ingredients (and raw, to boot), it takes no time at all to make. And you can either serve it out of a larger scooped melon or serve it in smaller scooped melons for an extra special presentation. Serve after dinner before the dessert course.

1 small seedless watermelon

1 small cantaloupe

2 tablespoons lemon juice

Fresh mint, for garnish

1. Wash and dry the melons and cut each in half. Using a melon baller, scoop out 10 large watermelon balls and 10 large cantaloupe balls. Place in a small bowl.

2. Scrape out any remaining watermelon and cantaloupe, reserving all 4 halves of the melons, and blend in a food processor for 1 minute. Add the lemon juice and blend again for 4 minutes on high. Pour the "soup" into the reserved watermelon and cantaloupe "bowls." Add 5 melon balls to each bowl. Garnish with fresh mint.

GRILLED FRUIT

Caramelized fruit is so delicious especially on a hot summer's day. If you don't have a grill you can use a skillet and get the same grilled effect. Serve with soy whip, or Coconut Whipped Cream (see page 13), and a sprig of mint.

2 medium peaches

2 medium plums

20-ounce can pineapple rings, drained

1 cinnamon stick

½ cup light agave

1. Wash and dry the peaches and plums. Cut in half and remove the pits. Place in a bowl and add the pineapple, cinnamon stick, and 4 cups cold water. Let the fruit soak for 10 minutes.

2. In a large greased skillet, cook the fruit over medium–high heat, only adding the cinnamon stick to the pan when the fruit is almost done, after 10 minutes. Turn the fruit over after 5 minutes.

3. Drizzle the fruit with the agave before serving.

PEPPERMINT BARK

This is one of my mother-in-law's favorites. Placed into decorative bags tied with ribbon, I give it out as a holiday treat to family.

1 cup chopped organic peppermint candies

3 cups vegan chocolate chips, tempered (see page 132)

1. Place the peppermint candies into a food processor and process on high speed for 10 seconds, or until crushed into small pieces. Set aside.

2. Pour the tempered chocolate onto a parchment-lined cookie sheet and spread into an even layer. Sprinkle the chopped peppermint on top.

3. Once the chocolate has hardened, after about 15 minutes, break it into uneven shapes using your hands. Store in an airtight container for up to 2 months.

TOFFEE SQUARES

Who doesn't like toffee? These squares are so easy—and so sinfully delicious that I have to stop myself from eating the whole tray! This is a great dessert to bring to a party.

2 sleeves saltine crackers

1 cup butter substitute

¾ cup light brown sugar

12 ounces gluten-free chocolate chips

1. Preheat the oven to 350°F.
2. Line a 10x15-inch cookie tray with crackers in a single layer.
3. In a medium saucepan, melt the butter substitute and brown sugar over low heat. Pour evenly over the crackers and bake for 6 to 8 minutes.
4. Remove the tray from the oven and sprinkle the chocolate chips over the bubbling toffee squares. Once the chips are melted, spread the chocolate evenly. Cool completely, for about 1 hour, and cut into squares. Store in the refrigerator for up to 7 days.

SPICED PECANS

Another classic recipe from my childhood, my mom, grandmom, and aunts make these delicious pecans around the holidays. Perfect in a Mason jar with a ribbon for a gift, the buttery pecans mixed with cinnamon sugar are to die for.

1 cup evaporated cane juice

1 teaspoon cinnamon

1 teaspoon salt

1 pound pecan halves

1½ teaspoons egg replacer, whisked with 2 tablespoons warm water

1. Preheat the oven to 200°F.

2. In a large bowl, mix the cane juice, cinnamon, and salt.

3. In a small bowl, stir the pecans with the egg replacer. Add to the large bowl and toss well. Spoon into a 9 x 13-inch baking pan.

4. Bake for 1 hour, stirring every 15 minutes. Store in a glass jar or airtight container. The pecans can be frozen for up to 6 months.

PRETZEL RODS

A very popular dessert at my retail kiosks, the sweet and salty mix of pretzels and chocolate is so tasty. The combinations are endless when making these, as you can see from the three different toppings below. Get creative!

24 pretzel rods

1½ pounds chocolate chips, tempered (see page 132)

1 cup finely chopped chocolate sandwich cookies

1 cup unsweetened shredded coconut

2 cups dried cranberries

1 cup chopped pistachios

1. Have your bowl of tempered chocolate at hand. Take a large piece of foil or wax paper and line your counter. Make separate piles of each topping: the finely chopped cookies, the shredded coconut, the dried cranberries, and the chopped pistachios.

2. Dip 2 pretzel rods together at the same time into the bowl of chocolate and, using an offset spatula, spread the chocolate onto the rods, making sure to leave an inch at the top of the pretzels for a handle. Remove any excess chocolate.

3. Place the chocolate-dipped pretzel rods onto the topping of your choice. Cover the entire chocolate part of the pretzel with the topping and then transfer to the piece of foil or wax paper to dry. Repeat with all the pretzel rods and toppings.

4. The pretzel rods will keep for 2 months in an airtight container.

TEMPERING CHOCOLATE AND MAKING CHOCOLATE CUPS

Once you have the principles down for tempering chocolate you can make so many great desserts. Like these chocolate mousse cups—supereasy and everyone will ask, "How did you do that?"

Small stovetop pot
Medium stainless-steel bowl
4 cups vegan chocolate chips
Large piece of foil or wax paper
5 small round balloons

1. First add 1 cup of water to a small stovetop pot and bring it to a simmer over medium heat. Place 3 cups of chocolate chips into a medium stainless-steel bowl and place the bowl on top of the simmering pot. Continually stir the chocolate until it is 80 percent melted. Take the bowl off of the stove and dry the bottom of it, making sure no water gets into the melted chocolate. Continue stirring off the heat, until the chocolate is completely melted.

2. Add the remaining cup of chocolate chips and stir until melted. The more you stir the better. This agitates the crystals in the chocolate and allows for the chocolate to dry quickly and snap when you bite into it.

3. Once all of the chocolate is melted, test it with your finger. If the chocolate is cool to the touch, put a small amount on a piece of foil. If it hardens and is shiny within 2 to 3 minutes, it is in temper. If it does not harden, continue to stir and add another ounce of chocolate, stirring, until it is melted. Repeat until the chocolate is in temper.

4. Blow up 5 balloons and dip each into the tempered chocolate. Shake each balloon after dipping to remove excess chocolate. Place on a parchment-lined cookie sheet and let dry for approximately 10 minutes. Once dry, pop the balloons with a knife and remove each balloon from the bottom of each cup.

5. The cups can now be filled with Chocolate Mousse (see page 134) or Coconut Whipped Cream (see page 13) and fresh fruit.

CHOCOLATE MOUSSE

 SERVES 5

My delicious chocolate mousse is made with melted chocolate for a rich and decadent flavor. Spoon or pipe into chocolate cups and serve with fresh raspberries and mint for a very easy but beautiful dessert for a special occasion.

28 ounces soft tofu, cubed and drained

2 cups gluten-free chocolate chips

8 ounces tofu cream cheese, at room temperature

½ cups tofu sour cream

1 cup organic powdered sugar

¼ teaspoon xanthan gum (optional)

5 chocolate cups (see page 132)

1. In a food processor, blend the tofu at high speed, stopping and scraping down the sides of the machine every minute for 3 minutes, or until the tofu is creamy in texture. Meanwhile, melt the chocolate in a microwave-safe bowl at 75 percent power until softened, about 1 minute 30 seconds, stopping and stirring after each 30-second interval. Turn the food processor to low speed and pour the melted chocolate into the bowl. Mix for 2 minutes, stopping and scraping down the sides of the bowl, until well combined.

2. Using a stand mixer, beat the cream cheese until smooth, about 1 minute. Stop and scrape down the sides of the bowl and add the sour cream, powdered sugar, and xanthan gum, if using. Mix on medium-high speed for 1 minute. Then, add the chocolate tofu mixture to the bowl and blend on high for 1 minute.

3. Cover with plastic wrap and refrigerate the chocolate mousse for 30 minutes before piping into the chocolate cups. The mousse will keep for 1 week in the refrigerator.

TIRAMISU

 SERVES 8

Tiramisu means "pick me up" in Italian. In my vegan version, I use Marsala wine instead of rum, which adds such a nice flavor. I sell this in restaurants and most people don't even know it's vegan and they love it. The alternating layers and flavors go together so well.

1 cup butter substitute, at room temperature

1½ cups evaporated cane juice

2 teaspoons vanilla extract

3 cups unbleached flour

4 teaspoons baking powder

6 teaspoons egg replacer, whisked with 8 tablespoons warm water

1 cup soy milk

1 tablespoon white vinegar

COFFEE FILLING

2 cups strong black coffee

¼ cup Marsala sweet wine

Cream Cheese Frosting (page 66)

Shaved chocolate, for finishing

1. Preheat the oven to 350°F. Grease and flour a 10 x 15-inch cookie sheet.

2. Using a stand mixer, beat the butter substitute, cane juice, and vanilla extract at medium speed until combined. Stop and scrape down the sides of the bowl, increase the speed to high, and whip the mixture until light and fluffy, about 2 minutes.

3. In a small bowl, mix the flour and baking powder. In a separate bowl, combine the egg replacer, soy milk, and vinegar. Alternate adding the dry and wet ingredients, starting and ending with the dry ingredients, to the mixer bowl, beating for 10 seconds after each addition. Stop and scrape down sides of bowl, making sure all the butter substitute is incorporated. Beat for 30 seconds on medium speed. Spread the batter evenly onto the prepared cookie sheet.

4. Bake the cake for 20 to 25 minutes, or until a toothpick inserted in the center of the cake comes out clean. Cool the pan on a wire rack for 10 minutes, then flip the pan over to release the cake. Cool for another 45 minutes.

5. While the cake is baking, brew the coffee. Let cool, then add the Marsala. Set aside.

6. Once the cake has cooled, cut it into 3 even sections. Place the first layer onto your serving dish and prick it all over with a fork. Using a pastry brush, liberally dab the coffee mixture onto the cake. Spread a third of the cream cheese frosting and sprinkle with a third of the chocolate shavings. Repeat 2 more times. Store the tiramisu in the refrigerator for up 5 days.

CHOCOLATE STRAWBERRY TRIFLE

 SERVES 4

This is a lighter version of my chocolate mousse with chocolate pudding mix for a fluffy texture. Mix with strawberries, chocolate graham cracker crust, and chocolate drizzle for a really sweet treat.

GRAHAM CRACKER CRUST

24 Chocolate Graham Crackers (page 102)

¼ cup evaporated cane juice

½ cup butter substitute

CHOCOLATE FILLING

14 ounces firm tofu

¼ cup cocoa powder

One 3.8-ounce package organic chocolate pudding mix

½ cup tofu sour cream

2 cups strawberries

½ cup melted gluten-free chocolate chips

1. FIRST MAKE THE CRUST: In a food processor, finely crush the chocolate graham crackers, about 2 minutes. Place in a medium bowl and add the cane juice. In a microwave-safe bowl, melt the butter substitute in the microwave for about 30 seconds. Add to the graham crackers and cane juice, stir, and set aside.

2. NEXT MAKE THE CHOCOLATE FILLING: Using a food processor, blend the tofu until smooth, stopping and scraping down the sides of the bowl as necessary, for about 2 minutes. Add the cocoa powder, pudding mix, and sour cream. Blend on high speed for 2 minutes, until well combined.

3. Wash and dry the strawberries and cut into ¼-inch-thick slices. Set aside.

4. Using glass serving dishes, alternate layering the graham cracker crust with the chocolate filling and strawberries. Top each trifle with some drizzled melted chocolate.

RESOURCES

MAGAZINES

VegNews
An award-winning vegan magazine and website packed with recipes, travel, news, food, and reviews; promoting animal rights and vegetarian ethics.
www.vegnews.com

Vegetarian Times
Delivers simple, delicious food, plus expert health and lifestyle information that is exclusively vegetarian.
www.vegetariantimes.com

ANIMAL ADVOCACY GROUPS

Farm Sanctuary
Farm Sanctuary is an American animal protection organization, founded in 1986 (and originally funded by sales of vegetarian hot dogs at Grateful Dead concerts) as an advocate for farm animals. It promotes laws and policies that support animal welfare, animal protection, and vegetarianism/veganism by rescue, education, and advocacy. Farm Sanctuary houses over 800 cows, chickens, ducks, geese, turkeys, pigs, sheep, rabbits, and goats at a 175-acre animal sanctuary in Watkins Glen, New York.
www.farmsanctuary.org

Compassion Over Killing
COK is a nonprofit animal advocacy organization based in Washington, D.C. Working to end animal abuse since 1995, COK focuses on cruelty to animals in agriculture and promotes vegetarian eating as a way to build a kinder world for all of us, both human and nonhuman.
www.cok.net

Mercy For Animals
Mercy For Animals is a non-profit animal rights organization focused on promoting a vegetarian diet.
www.mercyforanimals.org

United Poultry Concern
A national non-profit animal rights organization that addresses the concerns over the treatment of domestic fowl, including chickens, ducks, and turkeys in food production, science, education, entertainment, and human companship situations. The organization was founded by animal rights activist and writer Karen Davis.
www.upc-online.org

NUTRITION & MEETING RESOURCES

Vegetarian Resource Group
A non-profit organization dedicated to educating the public on vegetarianism and the interrelated issues of health, nutrition, ecology, ethics, and world hunger. In addition to publishing the *Vegetarian Journal*, VRG produces and sells cookbooks, other books, pamphlets, and article reprints. VRG health professionals, activists, and educators work with businesses and individuals to bring about healthy changes in your school, workplace, and community. Registered dietitians and physicians aid in the development of nutrition related publications and answer member or media questions about the vegetarian and vegan diet.
www.vrg.org

EarthSave
Founded by "Diet for a New America" author John Robbins. A non-profit, educational organization promoting awareness of the health, environmental, and ethical consequences of food choices.
www.earthsave.org

BOOKS

Fast Food Nation by Eric Schlosser, Harper Perennial, 2002

Skinny Bitch by Rory Freedman and Kim Barnouin, Running Press, 2005
www.skinnybitch.net

Vegan in 30 Days by Sarah Taylor, Taylor Presentations, 2008

Diet for a New America by John Robbins, HJ Kramer, 1998

MOVIES

Forks Over Knives
www.forksoverknives.com

Food Inc
www.foodinc.com

The Cove
www.thecovemovie.com

Fast Food Nation, 2006, Fox Searchlight

INDEX

 **ACKNOWLEDGMENTS**

I am so grateful to my Mom and Grandmom for showing me their love of baking and sharing it with me. I know they would be so proud of my accomplishments.

To my husband Paul, for his never-ending support and encouragement. Without you I wouldn't be where I am today.

To Gene, for all that you do for animals. Your tireless work on behalf of those who do not have their own voices is such an inspiration. I hope to be like you and give my all to better the treatment of all animals.

To Anja, your support and patience has made this experience so great. Thank you for believing in me and my desserts.